RK LAXMAN

Back with a Punch

EP UNNY

PAPER MISSILE

NIYOGI BOOKS

Published by
NIYOGI BOOKS
Block D, Building No. 77,
Okhla Industrial Area, Phase-I,
New Delhi-110 020, INDIA
Tel: 91-11-26816301, 26818960
Email: niyogibooks@gmail.com
Website: www.niyogibooksindia.com

Editor: K.E. Priyamvada
Layout: Shashi Bhushan Prasad
Cover design: Anurag Hira
Cover illustrator: Douluri Narayana

ISBN: 978-93-91125-27-1
Publication: 2022
Reprint: 2025

Publisher's note: Every effort has been made to ensure the accuracy of the information presented in this book. The images used in this book come from either the public domain or from the public commons, unless otherwise stated. The publisher welcomes comments and feedback from readers, in order to improve future editions, at niyogibooks@gmail.com.

Printed at Niyogi Offset Pvt. Ltd., New Delhi, India

To

Sundar Ramanathaiyar
(1953–2016)
&
Abheek Barman
(1967–2019)

CONTENTS

INTRODUCTION

To begin wide-eyed at the very beginning was grace. R.K. Laxman started newspaper cartooning just in time to record the birth of the nation in 1947. The baptismal cartoon in *The Free Press Journal* has PM Nehru as a photographer coaxing a distressed boy sitting amidst studio props to smile—a task the country's cartoonists eventually took over.

If the timing was perfect, the placement was no less. Oddly enough, it was not the capital, Delhi that gave Laxman his big breaks, but Mumbai. He warmed up here at *The Free Press Journal* and went into an ultra-marathon at *The Times of India*.

Cartoons have a history of growing with cities and Mumbai was a city waiting for its cartoonist. Laxman stepped in to find a willing mass of newspaper readers battling everyday issues. His cartoons told them that the chaos was common to all; there was nothing personal about it and added, for good measure, that much of the chaos was thanks to the rulers in faraway Delhi. That extra disdain for the national capital and its self-centred politics sharpened the wicked pencil. The cartoon bonded with the metropolis and eventually with every new city to which the newspaper reached out.

The print cartoon was already a scattered presence in India by the late 19th century. Like cricket, it came with the British and, as in the US, had a head start over cinema. 'Funnies before movies' is how an American cartoon historian put it. The young American nation celebrated the comics and developed it into an industry. India took to the alien visual satire at its own pace. Here it took a while for anything like a critical mass of cartoon readership to emerge. That happened around Laxman. Even so, his fans remained mute loyalists for want of an ecosystem to applaud, unlike cricket fiends and film buffs who get upfront about their favourites, pick up trivia and reel off statistics. Comic art fans behave precisely like this overseas—wherever the work practice has been organized into archives, shows, talks, galleries and museums. We have so far managed to build one museum for cartoonist Shankar near his hometown in Kayamkulam, Kerala, and the rest is history waiting to be made. We let our democracy and cartoons fend for themselves.

Meanwhile, across our English and the language press, new generations of cartoonists keep coming up. Evidently there is readership and it could finally be changing right before our eyes. More and more Indians are turning visually literate and are accessing the Internet, which features a fine spread of comics from the world over. For the first time a large number of comics-savvy readers are looking at our news cartoons. More irreverent eyes, therefore, could be watching our politics, which is what mainly drives the Indian cartoon. Also, political acts could be increasingly seen as personal.

Not that conventional readers are unaware of these trends, but they are used to following the news cartoon with one eye and the comics with another. Such ocular acrobatics are no longer necessary. Comic art is converging globally into a broad spectrum that encompasses all things comic—the animated image, cartoonish video, graphic novel, cartoons and comic strips on print and the web. The Japanese were lucky to have coined a common name for all things comic, 'manga', before the crossovers happened.The best of newsrooms the world over are factoring in the broadening domain of the cartoon. Editors are no longer content with any space-filling illustration. They commission cartoonists to create visual essays and graphic reportage that add editorial value.

Our own cartoon watchers are no longer passive. Many are developing an active interest and some have become enthusiasts. In the process, what happens to a veteran like Laxman? He started off with a World War Two vintage skill set that stood him well through an extra long career. He never bothered to innovate or update, but stuck to his seasoned style with the same loyalty with which he bought and drove his black Ambassador cars. Always Ambassador, always black. Would he fade away, which is nothing unusual for the best of the lot in this perishable practice? No sign of that. On the contrary you see him back on the web, rerun by old loyalists and shared by young netizens.

This book tries to find out why and it hasn't been easy. Not that Laxman was particularly reticent or as silent as the Common Man he created. This cartoonist did speak, but from memory. He never wrote a diary or kept notes, rarely wore a watch and certainly didn't look at the calendar. He created a book-length autobiography with few events dated. And when he sat down for an interview, he stopped where he wanted to. The man was no biographer's delight. But he left clues, most of which are in that erstwhile princely state now called Mysuru. That is where Laxman grew up. No cartoonist is born in a vacuum. Multiple influences, personal and political, go into the making of this hybrid art practice.

Once you follow him from Mysuru to Mumbai, the cartoonist recedes and the cartoon takes over. Then on, there is no dearth of eloquence. The Laxman cartoon speaks, years after his death with undimming clarity and a new-found relevance. Intriguingly, it speaks with an enhanced punch.

MYSORE: COW AND THE CROWS

One failure can make a success. It takes two to make a star. R.K. Laxman failed twice in his attempt to get ahead in life. We are immensely glad he did. Or we wouldn't be talking today, years after his death, about this remarkable practitioner of a newspaper art, known for its fleeting impact.

Laxman failed to get into a proper art school and went on to become the country's best regarded cartoonist. Not before he ran into a second big shock. The best workplace turned him down—New Delhi, then the new capital of a young and bustling democracy. That in turn made him set up shop in one of the most vibrant cities in the world. Mumbai made him what he was and looks like remaking him for an emerging generation of young Indians. In news cartooning the world over, the best of cartoonists are read, liked and celebrated in their lifetime and then, at best, recalled on occasion. Laxman seems to be destined for a fuller afterlife.

The life lived is hard enough to chronicle, a good part of it having been lived unseen within the walls of a corner office in Mumbai's *Times of India* building. Six hours daily for six days a week over 68 years, the country's favourite cartoonist vanished into his cabin. To understand this private, complex workaholic who routinely reduced the day's news clutter to a chuckle, you have to look all over for random clues. For sheer convenience, we might as well begin at the beginning.

The Much-mentioned NO

In the not-so-eventful princely state of Mysore, now called Mysuru, where he was born and brought up, the first event that marked Laxman's life was his failure to get into the celebrated JJ School of Arts in Mumbai, which has since been much mentioned. No write-up, intro or blurb on the cartoonist is complete without it. This is so because the story in retrospect lends itself to retelling; it has a dramatic twist sweetened by revenge at the end. Decades after rejection, the art school invited the celebrity cartoonist to preside over its annual painting competition. Laxman could have quietly returned after giving away the prizes. The organizers insisted on a speech and got what they asked for. The chief guest thanked the institute for making him what he was, a cartoonist. Had they admitted him when he applied, he said, he would have ended up as a full-fledged visualiser in an ad agency, promoting mosquito repellents.[1]

For the boy who loved to sketch, the best part of schooling was the drawing teacher from Maharashtra, dressed in a silk suit, turban and all, munching scented betel nut. The master was trained at JJ School of Arts. He was reputed enough for young Laxman to convince his liberal, yet conventional, household that an art diploma from this school was as good as a university degree. He would at least have a career in advertising. Uneasy with the school curriculum, the backbencher saw the art course as a relief from the bigger boredom that awaited him at the university.

After high school, when it was time to seek admission to JJ School, he had piled up enough art work to send across. After a wait that lasted endless weeks the reply came. It was a 'no' that cited inadequate entry level skills. It was enough to shake the starry eyed youngster who was already a locally liked prodigy. As a child, Laxman was prone to take things to heart and break down. His autobiography in the early pages has such teary instances every five pages or so. It has as many instances of bouncing back too. Making pictures was by then second nature to the boy. He had graduated from the homebound scrawling on any flat surface to compulsive doodling on notebooks in the classroom.

He had already secured the first recognition, which came from his mother. On a crucial forenoon she saw on the floor a scrawl in chalk of a bald head that bore a striking resemblance to her spouse, Rasipuram Krishnaswamy Iyer, the venerable headmaster of the local high school. Between the two, not without an argument, the couple decided not to wipe it off. Laxman's mother Gnanambal read widely, was good at tennis and bridge and played chess with Mysore's Queen. She had what it took to prevail over her stern husband.

By evening the five siblings had an eyeful of the youngest brother's pictorial take on their father. It stayed on to entertain visitors for several weeks before it finally faded out. Laxman's was an easy home to grow up in. There weren't too many dos and don'ts. At some stage, his older brother R.K.Narayan, already a published author, was asked to guide the budding artist, who was a good 15 years younger. The mentoring didn't go beyond the periodic reminder that a handkerchief was a better option than the front of his shirt for wiping pencil and chalk stains.

At school, like all budding cartoonists, the student had the mandatory brush with the teacher, with a vital difference. The usual story has the kid drawing the teacher's face and getting caught, whereupon ears get tweaked or on that rare occasion the back gets patted. Either way the rite of passage is done. Here, Laxman had just doodled the figure of a tiger on the margins of the note book. The Maths teacher sighted it and blew his top, seeing it as his own caricature. This was farthest from the student's mind but nobody believed it because the resemblance was uncanny. Caricaturing is inherently provocative, sometimes more than the cartoonist wants to be. Once a rough sketch is seen as a cartoon, the touchy viewer can read just about anything into it. Decades later in a far more advanced India, Laxman's cartoons faced similar overzealous readings by the official censor.

From early on Laxman worked hard to develop a style that was guaranteed to please readers and frustrate analysts. The latter dissect and when they can't find an easy answer, they dissect even more. And Laxman provides enough to probe. Many little things add up to make his cartoons what they are. If there is such detail, the devil can't be far. Why so many animals and birds in a political cartoon? What is that goat doing in the background? Why is the crow looking too defiant? Such were the doubts that plagued the censor under Indira Gandhi's Emergency regime. It is customary in every culture to use animal metaphors to praise or deride. When the cartoonist does it, the effect somehow amplifies.

As recent as 2018, in the non-censoring India, the Madras High Court had to restrain legislators who took offence to a cartoon in a popular Tamil newspaper *Dinamalar* that depicted them as monkeys. After dismissing the charges against cartoonist Karna and upholding the cartoonist's right to ridicule, Justice G.R. Swaminathan made the broader point that animals have 'intrinsic worth and value' as much as humans, and there is no derision in comparing the two. 'Apes are after all our primitive ancestors. They are our distant cousins. Our culture sees divinity in every aspect of nature. Hanuman the monkey god is a hero as well as a venerated deity.... Man occupies a higher spot in the evolutionary hierarchy. But, that does not make him superior to others. This is because, in the natural scheme of things, one is integrally linked to every other.'[2]

Laxman hardly ever went to the extent of actually reducing public figures to animals or birds. But his work did have its share of fauna. He would scatter them in his pictures, making you wonder what he was up to. This noncommittal impishness was key to his humour. The concluding remarks of the judge, made in a different context, seem to resonate with Laxman's art that took an extended interest in forms beyond the human. He inked in all things that flew, hopped and crawled, not to mention the windswept dried leaf. His lifelong fascination for the crow is thanks to the impartial non-anthropocentric gaze the judge talked about. Before he eventually sketched and painted individual crows in characteristic postures and launched a parallel career as a painter, the winged creature was invariably part of the cartoon's backdrop. The crow had a long journey that began in Mysuru.

The Urge to Include

Laxman retained this compulsive urge to include, inconvenient for a workaday cartoonist. He never settled for minimalism, a pardonable practice in the pocket cartoon and common enough in big display cartoons. He had the art to draw nonstop without cluttering up the picture. It seemed as though he would have drawn some more had the block-maker not turned up to take away the art work. Back in his early cartooning days, visuals were replicated into metal moulds to print. Laxman's drawing was cut out for line printing, which demanded a fairly uniform spread of line art across the frame without much blank space. The good old block-makers were afraid that some stray patch of print ink would creep into the unattended blanks. If not with the censor, Laxman's style was in tune with the block-maker. The cartoonist used up most of the space with deft brushstrokes that left no scope for smudges or smears.

The happy result was a stop action shot of an everyday scene, which did full justice to the essential disorder that marks Indian spaces. This love for entropy, actually the fear of regimented order, kept Laxman from seeking work abroad, like Abu Abraham or Rajinder Puri. Forget work, he couldn't even vacation overseas extensively. He missed his daily dose of chaos. In the few weeks he was away in Europe, whenever he sat down to think up a cartoon in the setting he was in, he found the frame deprived and bereft of any drama. Everything was so much in place. No dog curled up on the steps, no cattle strayed in, no crow took flight. Once he returned to India and looked around all was well again. The frame came alive with a million micro-mutinies.

For the kind of situational humour Laxman sought to create, a familiar everyday situation had to be literally drawn out. In his daily cartoon column in *The Times of India*, 'You Said It', readers were treated day after day to a lifelike scene they could easily connect to. The key to cartoon appreciation is serial viewing. No matter how high the impact of a single cartoon, what sustains readership is habit, which is created by slotting the cartoon. To begin with 'You said it' appeared always on the top right corner of the front page. Eventually it began to float on page one but you couldn't miss it.

Over the days and weeks, these unconnected frames built up a kaleidoscopic continuity that sustained readers' interest. In the cartoon one day you saw a village school, next a factory floor, then a sprawling ministerial bungalow followed by half-built bridges and dug up roads. Altogether the everyday images added up to tell an endless tale of urban disquiet.

This is a considerable visual repertoire and Laxman seemed to have picked up most of it from Mysuru. At any rate, most templates were in place when he was finally ready to leave home. His hometown was his lab. Strangely a bigger southern city like Chennai didn't fascinate him. Partly because his mother took him there in summer, when the port town simmers. Even so, there must have been a lot there a child could fall for—the long sandy beach, cinemas, statues, temples, the tramway and a big harbour. Nothing worked. He was happy to return to the cooler and cosier Mysuru. There was a similar hold the town had over R.K. Narayan, his writer brother. The author stayed on there through the best part of his working life. He sat down at home during the day to write and went out for long walks in the evening.

'If Mysore didn't have such long roads, Narayan's prose wouldn't have been so unhurried,' wrote bureaucrat, writer and townsman H.Y. Sharada Prasad.[3] Even as it shaped a writing style, the town nurtured drawing skills. It wasn't long before the young cartoonist was locally noticed. The erstwhile princely state of Mysore prided in art, culture and education, apart from being remarkably westernized. Laxman had participated in a couple of art shows and won a prize for a series of pencil sketches of his toddling nephew.[4]

Discovering 'Cow'

Having coped with the JJ school rejection, Laxman kept working on his drawing. There wasn't a single day when he didn't sketch. He didn't buy into the convenient fallacy that if you can't draw too well, you can cartoon. Any such thought would have been banished because the first cartoonist who caught his eye and whose signature he misread as 'Cow' was the very best in the business.[5] Laxman's father, an avid reader, subscribed to a host of English publications, including *The Hindu* newspaper. Little did he anticipate that the funny picture on the paper's op-ed page would change his son's life. The syndicated cartoon was by *Evening Standard's* David Low, Fleet Street's star. The signature was the only part of the drawing that was casual enough to be misread. Much reflection went into the art work.

Low was a master draftsman and a known connoisseur of Renaissance painting. His composition and caricatures were well thought out and brush strokes rehearsed. Evidently the look and feel of the printed picture captured the Mysuru boy more than the content driven by politics that was hardening around a man called Hitler. Unaware of such guile yet, Laxman simply knew he wanted to be a cartoonist like 'Cow' and to be so, he must draw well. If art school refused to teach him, he must teach himself. His leisure then on was split between cricket and art.

Whenever he wasn't holding a bat or lobbing a ball for the 'Rough and Tough and Jolly Team' he captained, he was sketching. Weekdays he sat in best friend H.K.'s room at his house and sketched whatever I saw through the window.'[6] He learned looking out the window and it became his work practice. Weekends he cycled with easel, brushes and paint to the rocks, streams and the ageless trees of Mysore. The princely state's capital was big enough to explore but not too big to lose sight of its prodigy. The fact that his family was part of the town's elite helped. But at least once access to the powers got a bit too close for comfort. One night a cavalryman rode up with a royal commission that commandeered the budding artist to fill up one whole wall of a kindergarten school with a mural. Hardly an assignment for a schoolgoer. The palace had evidently overestimated the age of the published artist. The student could explain and cry off without attracting royal displeasure.

Laxman took his time to enter college. At the final school exam, he failed the Kannada language paper by five marks and had to wait a whole year to do the re-exam and qualify for admission. However his art work had preceded him to the university. Even while in school, he was invited to illustrate articles in the college magazine. He was already noticed for his sketches that accompanied his brother R.K. Narayan's acclaimed early novel *Swamy and Friends* and short stories, which *The Hindu* newspaper from Chennai featured regularly. The published child artist was beginning to earn too. Enough for a masala dosa and coffee at the café and a weekly movie show.

While the movie hall typically ran silent films accompanied by a live pianist, the town's bookstore was way ahead of its times. Unwittingly so. Far from the humbling multitude of tomes packed into high book shelves, the little room was a brick and mortar version of today's online bookstore. Krishna & Co had near zero inventory, a single book shelf mostly empty, and a proprietor who was networked enough to get you your book in a couple of days. While a set of art history titles ordered by a local library lay waiting to be delivered, Laxman and a friend were allowed a good long look. 'Mr Krishna was generous enough to delay the delivery till we had finished going through the six bulky volumes.'[7]

Thanks to these small town graces, by the time he was in college, Laxman had found his calling. He was rigorously training in water colour, oil, pen and ink. After picking up a university degree as a familial obligation, he was determined to pursue an art career. How or when this pursuit got narrowed down to newspaper cartooning isn't clear. In fact his autobiography and interviews offer reflections and impressions, hardly any dates and names. The art teacher who mentored him is a vivid picture in colourful silk with even a waft of scented betel nut thrown in, but is nameless. His best friend's privacy can't be better preserved; he is no more than 'H.K.' in the autobiography. Later in a face to face interview with Karan Thapar, Laxman slipped in the full name, 'H. Krishnaswamy'.[8]

What else do you expect from the creator of an Everyman protagonist who had the pride of place on the front page of a major newspaper, but didn't utter a word in half a century? Laxman confesses in his autobiography that he is relying 'on his rather feeble memory,' adding, 'I'm not in the habit of keeping notes about any event, big or small.'[9] He doesn't dedicate his autobiography to his parents but to 'the memory of my parents'. So when you follow him, he will only take you as far as his memory goes. Beyond that you are on your own. When you search for answers to questions, such as how the resilient artist on the rebound turned to cartooning, don't expect helpful answers. Watch out for dots to join.

TO MUMBAI VIA FLEET STREET

In Mysuru, the young Laxman was doing too much art for a cartoonist. The cartoonist in the making was practising like a regular art student—landscape, human figure, still life, besides anatomy lessons he himself devised to study gestures and postures with a mirror. He had also mastered a range of drawing tools from chalk, pencil, charcoal, pens and brushes. The output included black and white line art, shaded pencil sketches, paintings in water colour as well as oil. This is a surplus skill set for a cartoonist,who by temperament is an artist in a hurry, content to find a decent functional line that can quickly do the day's work and move on. True to the original use of the word—'cartoon' meant the basic preparatory drawing—the daily cartoonist wouldn't tarry too much on art. The core activity is picking the day's top news, processing it into a visual and narrowing down on a good gag before the dreaded deadline. When he settled down to regular cartooning, Laxman routinely exceeded this brief. For him the day's work wasn't complete without that extra bit of detailing.

The Second Specs

An Indian cartoonist who had a matching repertoire of surplus artistry was Mario Miranda. As compulsive a doodler as Laxman, soon after his early days as a child artist, he converted entirely into cartoonish mode, which eventually seasoned into the unmistakable Mario style. The switch isn't unnatural when you are hit by the mesmeric Searle. Ronald Searle was to Mario what David Low was to Laxman. More so for Mario because Searle's grip was visceral. When Laxman did live sketching, there was hardly any Low in it. The line art looked primarily like what it was intended to be, a sketch. Because there was a cartoonist at work, the drawing was perhaps a bit cartoonish, no more. The Low slant became evident only in the cartoons. Laxman's life studies of places and people bear more fidelity to the real unlike Mario's famed travel sketches, which are as stylized as his cartoons and yet give you a stunning sense of place. His cartoon characters, the office secretary Miss Fonseca, the minister Bundaldass, and Bollywood star Rajani Nimbupani, can all walk in and belong to his Goan landscapes and European sketches.

It would seem that Mario saw the world through a single comic cornea. Laxman instead took more than one look at the world. A second pair of glasses dangled from his neck. He sketched differently from the way he cartooned; there is no continuum between the drawing styles. His Common Man, very much part of the cartoon would stick out like an alien if photoshopped into his travel sketches. While he brought his rich experience of drawing from life into the cartoon, it was not without a clear comic shift in emphasis.

These niceties apart, there is no clue as to when exactly Laxman zeroed in on the cartoon as his prime pursuit and more vitally, how he picked up not just the form but the content of this newspaper art. At a live telecast in 2013, while receiving the lifetime achievement award from CNN-News18 IBN Channel, he indicated something like a defining moment. He said, 'The journey towards this event started when I was five...'

That could well have begun in his father's study. Laxman took his time to enroll in school and in that 'heavenly' pre-school phase, he had all day to roam about the house unsupervised. What caught his eye was the heap of pictorial English magazines in his father's study on the bedside table, mandatory reading for the English-knowing elite in colonial India. In the bunch he found *Punch*. He studied its comic drawings in pen and ink in multiple styles, undistracted by the text in English. He was too young to read and get the joke.

Finally, the cartoon as a form hit him when he sighted David Low on the op-ed page of *The Hindu* newspaper. The paper started carrying Low in 1933. The master was at his emergent best then. Laxman could have been as young as 12 when he had this contact high. You have to be precocious to be able to tune into a Low cartoon at that age. By the1940s, in his teens, Laxman had a better chance of figuring out the news and completing his understanding of Low, at his wartime best.

Back in Mysuru, however, the cartoon watcher betrayed no passion for the World War or national politics that was gathering momentum and impacting life closer home. With the war escalating, the Congress Party had sighted liberation from British rule. A mixed mood of expectancy was in the air country-wide, Mysuru included—of war-driven anxiety and the yearning for freedom. The young fan of David Low didn't betray any passion for student politics or for idolizing the national leaders. He seemed untouched by the customary highs of growing up then. For any early intimations of an astute political mind, look elsewhere.

When the 'Quit India' call came in 1942, Laxman was in bed with typhoid. He saw how history was being made from his sick bed. Not too distant a view. A good second-hand update came from his best friend H.K., who was part of the local bicycle brigade that agitated against the British Raj. H.K. eventually went to jail, where he was served soup that smelt of kerosene. This much was left uncensored in the letter from the student inmate that arrived with copious portions blacked out with a thick marker. This was Laxman's first physical view of censorship.

By then India's national politics was beginning to drive its political cartoon. Perhaps unnoticed by Laxman in Mysuru, cartoonist Shankar, a good 19 years older, was already halfway through his illustrious stint in *The Hindustan Times* in Delhi. This Keralite came to the capital from Mumbai, where he had found a day job in a shipping company and moonlighted for *The Free Press Journal* and *Bombay Chronicle*. He was more than a mere follower of news that was gathering pace.

His bachelor pad in Peddar Road was used to print the Congress Bulletin.[1]

However Shankar's student days in erstwhile Travancore, a princely state like Mysore, were spent without any known political activism. But in the state's capital Thiruvananthapuram, where he went to college, he must have surely sensed the doubly surcharged resistance in the air to both the British monarch as well as the local Maharajah. Politics was already beginning to radicalize in these parts, which the rulers sought to checkmate with selective reforms. Enough to eventually bring about several advanced social measures, such as temple entry for all Hindu castes and the abolition of the death penalty on 11 November 1944. The Republic is yet to catch up with the last.

In some respects, the princely state was benchmarking against the best of European states, even as its aspiring cartoonist was perfecting the very European art of defiance. Finally when he arrived in Delhi in 1932 to cartoon for the capital's premium paper *The Hindustan Times*, first under the editorship of Pothen Joseph and then Devdas Gandhi, Gandhiji's son, Shankar was thoroughly politicized and fully aligned to the freedom movement.

The younger Laxman went to work with no such political conditioning, though the Mysuru he grew up in was quite political. It couldn't have been otherwise. The place saw early industrialization and all that went with it including organised labour. In *The Indian Princes and Their States* Barbara N. Ramusack sums up the province:

> Because of its program of economic as well as administrative modernization, Mysore had one of the more sizeable industrial labour forces among the princely states...working class culture in Bangalore and the Kolar Gold Fields that generated public protests and private resistance...Workers organized substantial strikes beginning with the compositors at the Mysore Government Press in 1920, to the 18-day strike in the Kolar Gold Mines in 1930, to a 72-day strike at Bangalore textile mills in 1941, to two waves of strikes during the Quit India movement.[2]

Coincidentally Free India's two early cartoonists grew up in administratively progressive Hindu princely states not without their share of political turbulence. Hailing from upper caste Hindu families, both had access to all that came with such durbars including literacy, libraries and English education. But as cartoonists in the making they were shaped by the politics around them in quite different ways and this divergence set their work apart. So much so that by the 1960s and '70s, the country's newsrooms were divided between two schools of cartooning. The soft, appealing, everyday humour of a peerless Laxman versus the direct firebrand style of Shankar to whose flock was added for good measure practitioners as diverse as P.K.S. Kutty, O.V. Vijayan, Abu Abraham and Rajinder Puri. This delightfully simplistic binary continues to trigger much heated debate in media circles for want of any effort to create a broad scholarship in this art practice.

Guru David

The short point is that Laxman, who was ready to take up cartooning as a career in the politically surcharged 1940s, wasn't evidently political. Was he latently so? Ironically the only cartooning influence he acknowledged was David Low, which was much. The British master was a thoroughbred political creature. As the jewel in the colonial crown, India featured in his work often enough.

If not India, an Indian was already in world cartoons as a proponent of a bizarre concept of passive political resistance, Satyagraha. Gandhi loved the cartoon and loved to be in it.

Soon Gandhi became the visible index of Western media interest in India. By the late 1920s Low was regularly featuring Gandhi. In one iconic drawing captioned 'Passing Shadow', wrapped up in khadi robes the familiar figure was shown walking past the British PM's Downing Street residence, where delegates from every colony except India were meeting. This cartoon was among the lot that *Evening Standard* syndicated to British colonies including India and Sri Lanka. Laxman couldn't have seen this 1931 cartoon but Gandhi and India were very much there by the time he started following Low.

To begin with the drawing was what held the boy's attention, but somewhere down the line the rest of the cartoon would have cut across. More so, amidst a war that was turning global and driving news. Having famously anticipated Hitler's belligerence ahead of his government, Low was cartooning the World War with a certain authority. It is easy to fall for Low's art but you had to have an ultra tunnel vision to ignore the cartoon's intensely political statement, among the earliest public condemnations of Nazism.

No one follows a news cartoonist day after day for aesthetics. The content grows on you. In Low, rehearsed brush strokes and photographic caricatures went with the carefully arrived at comment. For the self-appointed student, it was exposure to editorial art at its best. Laxman never acknowledged any other cartoonist. David Low could well have been his sole guru.

Along with this self-devised art education, Laxman was a regular at the university. He dutifully followed the academic curriculum to please his parents. The small mercy from the classroom came in the form of the occasional history lesson that emphasized personalities more than chronology, trends and undercurrents. This was synergic to cartooning.

Sizing up personalities is part of political cartooning. Particularly for the Low disciple who would go beyond cardboard caricatures. Lesser cartoonists make do with functional scrawls that bear adequate resemblance to newsmakers. These are cartoonish by being less than portraiture, whereas a Low or a Laxman caricature is enhanced portraiture. Apart from bearing a resemblance, it tells you something about the person.

The process went beyond anatomical distortion. The public personality gets almost fictionalized to create a recurring characteristic impression.

When Low famously did his Hitler, he put this method to lethal use. He made the trademark moustache look like an accidental blot of ink on a perennially distempered face. The effect was comic and went completely against the super heroic awe-inspiring image the Fuehrer sought to invoke. Such a construct was pivotal to the Nazi scheme of things that projected a great fatherland around a grand leader. And here was an expat New Zealander in Britain vandalizing it all with a twirl of the brush. Hitler was furious. As the failed artist from Vienna, he knew how the visual hurts. Low was among the first ten on the Nazi hit list to be shot as soon as German troops entered London. Significantly, the cartoonist faced flak from sections of anti-Nazis as well for trivializing a cruel fascist to a clownish figure. This is the kind of risk you run when you do interpretative caricature. You could get hit from one to many sides.

Caricatures that Matured

Through less turbulent times, Laxman followed this school of mindful caricaturing more approvingly. He was praised for an early study of Nehru done in 1946, the same year *The Discovery of India* was published. The caricature could easily be grouped with the Bertrand Russell and T.S. Eliot he essayed on a visit to London, later. These drawings are on the lines of Vicky's caricatures that went with the *New Statesman* profiles of prominent personalities from outside the world of politics, like W.H. Auden, Orson Welles and Russell himself. The cartooning gaze here is no less irreverent but is as respectful as it could get. Nehru, the author, as portrayed here, eventually gave way to the PM who stayed on in fine form, till that fateful war with China was lost in 1962. Then on, the prime ministerial head was never held high in the Laxman cartoon. The defeated stalwart ambled in and out, often without the cap. He looked like a distracted version of his former self.

Though Laxman's considerable reputation was built around the pocket cartoon, where no public personalities or caricatures figured, his display cartoons marked newsmakers who ran the nation. In retrospect, they would give us a fine visual account of contemporary history. The action in the frame and the caption speak but more than the two the caricatures themselves add up to a story. You'll find how Jawaharlal Nehru, Indira

Gandhi, Atal Bihari Vajpayee, L.K. Advani, Sonia Gandhi and Rajiv Gandhi transformed through the years. Caricaturing at its best captures not just physical ageing but political seasoning. And when a politico like Morarji Desai remained too stiff to change, he was captured with matching static precision, ramrod straight and smile-less, unchanged through the decades. As Chief Minister of Bombay State, the venerable leader enforced prohibition and banned every sinful activity from horseracing to crossword puzzles. Mumbai seems destined to relapse into such periodic moral upsurge only to mercifully recover. Back in the 1950s too, the metropolis refused to become a monastery and its cartoonist stayed on to cheer.

RUSHING TO DELHI

When Laxman began cartooning in 1947, the best bet in the nascent democracy was the pair that led it. Gandhi and Nehru were known votaries of the free press and both loved the cartoon.

Nehru was friends with the capital's celebrity cartoonist Shankar. Barely a year into office in 1948 he inaugurated *Shankar's Weekly* in New Delhi with the much-mentioned call, 'Don't spare me Shankar!' Nehru's grace was predictable given the euphoric times, but Gandhi was steps ahead. He was the ultimate insider-outsider of the cartoon. He had caught the cartoonist's eye way back in his South African days. As early as 1907, *Sunday Times* in Johannesburg carried cartoons on Satyagraha, the new passive resistance he had launched against the Transvaal government. The coolie-barrister, as he was hyphenated in those intensely racist parts then, was not yet the cartoonist's delight—the easy to draw, bald, bespectacled figure, eventually simplified into a single flowing line by cartoonist Ranga. He appeared more formally and vividly as suited and booted, cap in place.

Even as he was being featured in cartoons, Gandhi harnessed the newspaper art as editor. He regularly reproduced in *The Indian Opinion*, the multi-lingual paper he brought out of Johannesburg, editorial cartoons from the British press. The cartoons were displayed without any Gandhian austerity. They were generously flashed across full pages and on occasion front paged.[1] By the time he returned to India, he had developed enough insight into the genre that he took on Shankar. He found a Shankar cartoon on Jinnah, not exactly a soulmate, offensive. 'You merely fulfill the first test of a cartoonist. Your cartoons are good as works of art,' he wrote to Shankar. He asked the cartoonist to speak accurately and ridicule without bite. He wrapped up the 80-word scribble on a postcard, as only he could, 'You won't resent this note. Yours Bapu.'[2]

Shankar didn't, but Laxman would've. 'Nobody tells me what to do,' he told Karan Thapar in a TV interview years later. But then his style would have provoked neither Gandhi nor Jinnah. After Shankar, the Indian cartoon got softer with Laxman before it hardened again in the hands of Rajinder Puri and O.V. Vijayan. Nothing is quite linear in our cartooning history. In any case it took decades for our politicians to get touchy enough to be offended by Laxman. He had no reason to fear the state in his formative years. On an early visit to Delhi, he sought and got five minutes of prime ministerial time. He left Nehru's office after a full hour. The PM walked the young cartoonist down to the steps of the Teen Murti House.

Such comfort between the ruler and its critic is at once priceless and problematic. One such celebrated bond in the last century was between Cuba's Fidel Castro and writer Gabriel Garcia Marquez. This however, happened across the laid-back literary space. To sustain warmth with an everyday irritant like the newspaper cartoon entails much patience. In India's early democracy the leadership either had plenty of it or it was too soon to shed pretences.

In any case, cartoonists couldn't have asked for more then. You only had to find a regular job. Laxman returned from Delhi without a plan and stopped over at Mumbai on his way back to Chennai. A couple of assignments came his way and he stayed back to complete one and then another till the inevitable happened. If you are cut out for a newspaper job, you can't be in Mumbai for long without being hired by *The Free Press Journal*, the gateway to legendary careers.

At the first regular cartooning job, he had company that shrunk soon. One of the two resident cartoonists, Bhat, left the job to become a hotelier. The other sat bent over the drawing board, chewing on his pipe. Bal Keshav Thackeray. According to author and veteran editor T.J.S. George, colleague Thackeray then was a pale shadow of his latter self.[3] He betrayed no signs of the firebrand politician he went on to become. He looked as regular a cartoonist as Laxman. Which then meant you modelled on David Low and expected Fleet Street-grade autonomy at work. Publisher Editor Swaminathan Sadanandhan had other ideas. He wanted his cartoonists to spare the star Communist leader S.A. Dange, who was a friend. Sadanandhan was no patch on Lord Beaverbrook, who tactfully ran the liberal David Low in the eveninger *Evening Standard* and the conservative Sidney Strube in the flagship *The Daily Express*. Sure enough, Mumbai's non-identical cartooning twins each went his own way. Thackeray hit the street to do his politics and Laxman caught a Victoria and rode in style to the *Times of India* office.

Illustrating the *Weekly*

Meanwhile, the birth of the nation went unrecorded by the one who had cartooned most vigorously for it. When the country was declared free, Shankar was between jobs. He had left *Hindustan Times* a year before freedom came and launched his weekly a year after. Laxman was lucky enough to record the moment of transition. He was still there at *The Free Press Journal* when the Union Jack came down but left soon after. He missed out on the crucial weeks of national coping that followed. The Brits had partitioned the subcontinent and left. We had our homeland to ourselves but there were many with no home or hope.

Bennet & Colman, the holding company of *Times of India*, had already hired Laxman but not as a cartoonist nor for its flagship. His assignment, to begin with, was at *The Illustrated Weekly of India* to illustrate features and do a comic strip for children. It took some years for him to move from the art department to the editorial section.

This was a painful wait, having honed the instinct to target the day's newsmaker in *The Free Press Journal*. This diurnal urge to needle the shakers and movers is basic to the art practice. That is what motivates the practitioners to do the daily grind. Some like Laxman shut themselves up and slave away for hours. Others, who are a lot less organized, rush in from the pub or golf course to the drawing board, work like one possessed against the advancing deadline, breast the tape and land the cartoon at the very last minute, even as the choicest of epithets escapes the news editor's lips.

In his early days as illustrator, Laxman found it hard to suppress the cartooning instinct. He struck up a deal with the editor for regular submissions with no assurance of publication. He would do a cartoon on alternate days; the editor looked at it, occasionally smiled and returned the original. The aspirant was probably being tested for an attribute more crucial to professional cartooning than draftsmanship—the ability to generate ideas regularly. The legendary Herblock got his first cartooning job thanks to his proven merit in ideating. His contributions as reader in a column in *Chicago Tribune* were noticed in press circles. Today we have a name for such contributors—citizen journalists. At *Chicago Daily News*, the editor told Herblock, 'Well, you don't seem to have any trouble coming up with ideas.'[4] One look at an early scrawl by Herblock or Laxman, you knew how well the rookie drew. The only thing to be ascertained was whether the bulb would flash on the next day and the day after.

After a decent pile of unpublished originals were created across months, Laxman finally made it to the group's eveninger. *The Evening News of India* carried his cartoon on the Berlin blockade of 1948. In a matter of weeks the cartoonist graduated to the front page of the flagship and into a punishing work schedule. He did three display cartoons a week and a three-in-one sum-up on Sundays. His position was formalized when the British owners of the holding company left and *Times of India* changed hands to the Thapars and then the Sahu Jain family. He was moved out of the art department into the editorial office of the Indianised *Times* as its first Chief Political Cartoonist.

Then on he stuck to a work routine he himself described as 'the life of a squirrel in a wheel cage'. With priestly rigour, he drove to work in a black Ambassador car, parked it precisely in the allotted slot in front of the office. He was in at 8.30 am, before anyone else showed up, shut himself up in his cabin till 5 pm when he would step out and drive back home before the evening traffic peaked. The break from routine happened only when he was on his annual holiday or out on a sketching assignment or during mandatory visits to Delhi.

Delhi Group Photo

The Chief Political Cartoonist wasn't living in the political capital, which was unthinkable then, and so he had to do the next best thing. He had to visit Delhi often enough to keep up with 'national' politics that was then made within the municipal limits of that old city. Laxman attended parliament sessions and observed leaders in action from the press gallery. This was a vital input in those days for a professional doodler. The Nationalist movement had thrown up one too many popular names and the cartoonist had to put a face to every one of these. And in those heady days of nationalism, despite the limited spread of newspapers and magazines and no TV, people knew Delhi's leaders as well as they knew Bombay's film stars. The Indian news cartoonists, unlike their counterparts in Europe or US, had to contend with a formidable variety of faces. Not just faces, as Abu Abraham used to say, even the hutments across the country look different from place to place.

Laxman, who leaned on the visual, had his job cut out. One saving grace was that most leaders were to be found in one place, the capital. This meant the cartoon frame had to constantly look like a group photograph. This was particularly so when the constituent assembly proceedings were on. There was a motley crowd of opinionated and vocal characters that no western cartoonist could have handled. Dr Ambedkar brought much needed relief when he turned in the draft of the Constitution. Politics moved from the Constituent Assembly to the cabinet and it became a wieldy group of usual suspects around the PM.

By then the cast around Nehru was getting limited and structured. The Prime Minister's circle was a far cry from Shankar's teeming festival crowd in the headydays of the independence movement. Nehru drew a different crowd from Gandhi and Laxman drew a different crowd from Shankar. Nascent nationalism was giving way to routine politics. With the early demise of Sardar Patel and Rajaji's break with the Congress, Nehru became lonelier at the top and Laxman may have breathed a sigh of relief. He could show the state at work without bringing in the entire jingbang. Nehru became the primary focus of Laxman's political cartoons..For instance, during the military action against the Portuguese in Goa, in 1961, Laxman drew a solo Prime ministerial figure bringing down an outsized hammer on a tiny rat!

The capital's navel gaze softened post-Nehru under the brief premiership of Lal Bahadur Shastri. For a while, it looked like power was getting shared and regional leaders were beginning to run the ruling party. You can trace the trend to the cartoon frame that was crowding up again. The short lived myth of collective leadership was, however, quickly busted by Indira Gandhi. She asserted her personal authority over party and government and brought Delhi back onto the centre stage. Laxman was to later reduce this phase to a much-cited cartoon where the umbrella-wielding PM is casually picking a chief minister for Andhra Pradesh from a long line of eager aspirants, mostly non-entities.

Till about the late 1980s, the cartoonist had to contend with newsmakers who either lived in the capital or were as good as residents. You find them in Laxman's cartoons, carting packed suitcases 'rushing to Delhi' or rushing back within hours of arriving from there. He had little love lost for the national capital. Not just because it refused him a job. He disliked the place on almost every liveability count. On short visits, he would ask, 'How do you guys live here, I say? How do you drive to work through extreme cold or intense heat?' The clockwork routine back in Mumbai between solitary confinement at work and the company of wife Kamala at home—to him 'harmonious existence'—seemed unthinkable in the differently chaotic Delhi. It is a difficult city that journalists loved because of access to centralized power and cartoonists for physical proximity to the powerful. The capital's cartooning edge was, however, over by the mid-1980s, when militant threats forced personal security guards to form rings around the VVIPs.

With their primary subjects out of sight, the capital's cartoonists had to source photographs and TV footage, just as their counterparts, elsewhere. This did impact the output, which increasingly became a string of images derived from equally flat images. A clear generational loss, it literally took one dimension out of the cartoon. Lost in the bargain was a certain raw power that marked the kind of caricatures Laxman and his peers developed from direct viewing.

Central Hall Caricatures

In the early days of free India, photographic caricaturing was in vogue. The likeness of character was central to it because you were dealing mostly with visually deprived readers. There was no national television and pictorial periodicals were few. Readers hardly saw anything beyond the grainy newspaper photographs of the leaders, many of which would be stock pictures the party office or the ministry doled out. The low visual literacy limited the scope of distortion in caricature which assumes a certain familiarity with the subject.

To arrive at this kind of safe caricature, it helped to study the movers and shakers from close quarters. Shankar had all the personal access he needed. Old timers have run into him at the corridors of Teen Murti Bhavan, the PM's residence. Yet he rigorously archived photographs of his subjects. He assigned professional photographers to record them through candid sessions to capture the fluid flow of face and hand. He must have had the biggest indexed photo collection of the country's who's who.

Shankar's prime disciple P.K.S. Kutty didn't follow a similar method nor did Laxman, who was very much his own man. Both must have made mental notes of what they saw from the press gallery and closer in the central hall of parliament. Ranga, another regular at parliament, didn't exactly wait to memorise but produced on-the-spot, slapdash sketches that grew into the largest pool of autographed caricatures, a world record.

The typical Laxman caricature was distilled from a range of memorised images—gesture, stance and mannerisms all in place. Having carefully arrived at this visual rendering, he couldn't always stick to it for long. India isn't an easy country, which lets you run a caricature for long. Our rulers are less steady and a lot more fluid than a Hitler, Churchill, Roosevelt or Stalin. Good or bad, they stuck to their politics. Ours is a polity far less settled than the British or American and our politicians constantly adapt, mutate and defect. Laxman had to keep up with signs of natural evolution as well as political mutation.

The first long-running Prime ministers were easy. Nehru was an open book. Indira Gandhi was half-shut and half-open, enough to manage. And her political transformations had drama. She brought out the best from cartoonists. If Laxman's cartoons on her were annotated and compiled they would make a political biography hard to beat. Caricaturing rarely got more dynamic. The wide-eyed novice; the wild dancer on an economic minefield; the street politician flinging stones at the oldies in the party; the overreacher brandishing a sword to taunt the statue of Justice; in retreat after an electoral upset, pushing her son Sanjay in a pram to the suburbs… Vibrant images that tell the story of an unsure loner who found her way in a man's world to power, more power and absolute power that eventually gave way to hubris, not before renewing a warm bond with the nation.

After such solid grounding on the prime ministerial watch, Laxman was stumped by a new face, when Rajiv Gandhi occupied the post. Here was this young strapping airline pilot who looked most pleasant and he was voted in with a mandate that exceeded Nehru's. Neither form nor content was lending itself to ridicule or caricature. To the cartoonist's relief, the young Rajiv Gandhi soon surrounded himself with colourful overzealous company that soon enough nudged him into serial bungling. The man became caricature-ready.

The cartoonist just has to wait. The best of leaders fall in line. How Laxman saw a range of PMs is best summed up in the August 1996 editorial cartoon he did to mark the start of the 50th anniversary of independence. The common man is nodding off in his familiar cane chair even as the TV in front is blasting off predictable tripe. There are 12 Prime ministerial pictures pinned to the living room wall. Lal Bahadur Shastri has a grin, Charan Singh a smirk. Eight others look grim. Nehru and Vajpayee alone smile. That was state of the nation for you, from a veteran of this wicked art.

COMMON MAN AND THE CROWN

Laxman readers tend to associate their favourite Common Man with the single-column pocket cartoon 'You said it'. Few realize that this is the character's second home. He came from the big bad world of the editorial cartoon.

Icons transcend the boring details of origin and growth but fans shouldn't miss out on the legacy. The Common Man first appeared in 1950 and can count as contemporaries the cast of two all time great comic strips—Peanuts born in 1950 and Dennis the Menace in 1951. Unlike Charlie Brown and Dennis, Laxman's man was never far from the world of news. There were no syndicating agencies or merchandising and licensing opportunities to sustain a comics industry in India. Indian cartoonists survived as newspaper employees and almost everything they did was news-driven. Laxman was no exception.

Long before TV, Laxman saw news as scenes playing out in the public arena. The cartoon wasn't complete without the viewers in the frame. You find a similar sprinkling of onlookers in the early Shankar cartoons as well. But the veteran quickly developed a privileged gaze that went with his location. This came naturally to the Delhi-based cartoonists who didn't merely view but witnessed news-making from a vantage point. Their comment had the stamp of authority that came from proximity. Laxman instead saw himself as a distant viewer from Mumbai, where there was no dearth of co-viewers. You just had to look around and you found a mini-India bustling past. Laxman picked his eager onlookers from this lot. The crowd in the cartoons eventually thinned down as national politics grew more Delhi-centric and distant to the Mumbai eye. Finally a lone figure stayed on. That was our familiar man in the checked coat.

Everyman has traditionally been used by dramatists to convey the moral of a story. This is a dicey device for the cartoonist, who should be anything but preachy. Laxman solved this problem brilliantly. His protagonist never spoke a word. The next challenge was to give the character a physical form that suggested a pan-Indian identity. Taking away the voice was easy, but one can't reduce the muted man to a matchstick figure to bypass all evident specificities. Given Laxman's maximalist style, the character had to be fleshed out. Again, it must connect to the whole of India, which was the news footprint the cartoonist surveyed every passing day.

In his 1950 appearance, the bespectacled figure was labelled in all caps as 'COMMON MAN' to dispel any specific identity.[1] One stand-out sign was the black cap he wore. Only certain classes of people in certain parts of the country wore a cap like that. The cap was kept aside whenever the Common Man switched to purely European clothes—suit, boots and baggy Chaplinesque trousers. It came back when he returned to the more regular Indian wear. Across the first Nehruvian decade the cap disappeared and reappeared much like the Prime Minister's own Gandhi cap. Whether there was a correlation is a matter best left to the researcher. Somewhere down the line the headwear vanished.

Common Man Finds a Second Home

By 1960 the little man settled down to what came to be recognized as his signature form. Wisps of hair over the ears, uncovered bald pate, round oversized glasses, checked coat and shoes without socks and to make his ethnicity suitably uncertain, the timeless unstitched Indian cloth called the dhoti—an attire common to many parts of the country. The protagonist had by then found its natural habitat—'You Said it'. 'My diligently-planned single-column feature', is how the cartoonist describes it in his autobiography.[2] Devoid of recognizable public personalities, Laxman revelled in the full freedom 'from the shackles of habitual realism, and indulged in a sort of political fantasy.'

The creator's unfettered joy didn't infect the creature. Unaware of his upgrade to freer ground, the common man carried on as befuddled as before, without a word. Mercifully silence wasn't a familial trait. Every once in a while, his wife joined him and she spoke her mind.

The Common Man went on to become the most recognizable Indian comic figure. Honoured with public statues in Pune and at Worli Seaface, Mumbai, and a commemorative postage stamp, he promoted Air Deccan, the country's first no-frills airline, as mascot. The standalone character's portability was evident early on and the creator was a beneficiary. Once, arriving late at night in Germany, on an invitation from Heidelberg

University, Laxman stepped out of the airport into dim-lit anonymity. He knew none and none knew him well enough to place him. As he looked around, up went a placard with the picture of the Common Man. The professor who had come to receive the cartoonist was suitably equipped.[3] The famously silent Common Man made the introductions.

The much interpreted silence has been broken once. In a sequential cartoon of 1954, the Common Man on an overseas visit is being harangued by a patronizing European on India's claim over Kashmir and Goa. After the long listen our man retorts, 'Supposing you tell me something about Kenya, Malaya, Cyprus…' The colonial relic beats a hasty retreat.[4] Again, contrary to popular impression, the man isn't always placid. He almost gets physical once. He steps on a button that activates a mechanized clenched fist that flies out of the microphone, hits and stops the speaker who is evidently going on and on.[5] The raw power of the hit is tempered by a mechanical interface. This goes well with the Laxman style of softening the blow, without pulling punches. The punch re-emerged after 23 years and how. You see the little man, sleeves rolled up, knocking out the grand old Congress party in the March 1977 elections that punished the ruling regime for the virtual one-party rule during the internal Emergency. This was the Common Man at his spirited best, the big citizen of a big democracy.

Barring the rare demonstrative surge, the man remains quiet. He seems to have yielded to the ways of the new state as early as the 1950s. You see him squatting on a bed of nails with yogic nonchalance or posing passively for a souped-up portrait by the budget-making finance minister. At the first Republic Day after Jawaharlal Nehru's death in 1965, the anxious ruling party made a gallant attempt to reboot the citizen. Laxman's response is a collector's item—a display cartoon where the Common Man appears twice. One of the two stood with the onlookers. The other occupied the pride of place on a decorated float driven by the new PM Shastri. This boost was as short lived as Shastri's prime ministership. Since then the Common Man broadly mirrored the Indian citizen's plunge.

Along this free fall from participation to passivity, Laxman's protagonist shows striking moments of resilience. Ahead of the professionally geared mountaineers, our man in common wear is clambering up Mount Everest, trying to catch up with soaring prices.[6]

Decades later he is back to volunteer for the manned mission to the moon. One of the scientists details the volunteer's impeccable credentials: 'This is our man! He can survive without water, food, light and shelter…' You could add, and 'his own hard-earned money'.

Taxed to the Bones

If there is anyone Laxman hated more than the terrorist it is the taxman. In 1962 on the war with China, the cartoonist blames Nehru as much for the wartime levies as the military setback itself. The PM is shown at the head of his feuding party appealing to the public to unite and sacrifice. The cartoonist is the down-to-earth householder of Mumbai and not the high-sounding critic of Delhi. The Common Man is seen at his worst whenever he is called upon to shell out tax. By PM Nehru in 1962, Rail Minister Prof Madhu Dantavade in 1977 and PM Deve Gowda in 1997. On each occasion the protagonist appears denuded, covering himself with the day's newspaper, having handed over all he has, including his clothes and shoes.

Laxman seems to suggest that the working Indian's mission in life is to earn enough to pay the state, go broke and get back to the grind to earn all over again for the next round of well-meaning taxes, levies and cess. It is an endless Karmic cycle of submission to the taxman. Seeing the state as an economic oppressor, as much as a political meddler, is the hallmark of advanced societies of Europe and the US. The IRS (Internal Revenue Service) is a pet target of American cartoonists. The ultimate inevitability of death and taxes is a common thread that runs through these cartoons.

The taxman often comes across in these drawings as the companion of the scythe-wielding Grim Reaper and when the cartoonist is very angry, as the reaper himself. Laxman comes close to first-world cartooning in his aversion to tax hikes. He is certainly not the only Indian cartoonist who scowls at the tax collector. But he has done it every time with extreme intensity, depicting his protagonist with not a stitch on him, in utter humiliation, risking his quiet dignity.

This is the voice of the self-made expat in a big city when the state touches his hard-earned income. The voice was back every morning to raise similar issues that mattered to an urbanizing India. The tone was far from respectful. Worse, it was getting popular. Trouble wasn't far.

The Crown that Clowned

The last decade of the last century a familiar Delhi leader emerged in a dramatic makeover. Measured, methodical and a longtime member of the Parliament's upper house, an unlikely L.K. Advani emerged as a shrill voice of faith-led populism. In 1990, he led a widely televised road show called Rath Yatra (Chariot Ride) through the Hindi hinterland in an automobile spruced up as a filmy chariot. Laxman met this campaign with a simple prop. He gave the big campaigner a small crown that looked straight out of calendar art. The kind that belongs to garish mass produced spreads of Indian mythological figures. In Laxman cartoons, Advani couldn't shrug off the ill-fitting headgear, even after he stepped out of the Toyota Rath.

The properly clad, familiar, lean, tall figure was shown donning this odd ornate crown through mundane everyday activities like parliamentary work, public meetings and diplomatic engagements. The incongruity was killing. And didn't go unnoticed by the leader's fans in journalism. More than a loose sally of admirers, Advani had a proper fan club in the capital, which saw a potential PM in their patron. A sudden buzz rose that cartoonist Laxman was losing his touch and must retire gracefully. Having done a great deal for Indian satire, he should now make way for youngsters, went the spiel. Younger cartoonists were no friends of Advani or his new avatar. Someone like Ravi Shankar was characteristically merciless. But none had the clout of Laxman. The worst fear of Advani fans was that the whole of Mumbai was behind its cartoonist. Political Delhi could no longer ignore Laxman, the prescient cityman.

After scoring a raw point on faith-led politics, Advani was looking for living room cheering. The last thing he wanted was appearance after crowned appearance in the cartoon alongside the sober, self effacing Common Man, the very picture of urbanity. The damage was cumulative over the days and weeks. There was no early resolution. Laxman took his time to dethrone the leader and the buzz died a natural death.

One lesson that emerged from this flutter was that more than individual cartoons the cartooning language itself was beginning to offend. A metaphor travelling through cartoons stung. Which meant something like a cartooning diction was emerging here and our leaders weren't liking it. At another level, the cartoon itself was finding synergy with cities and our leaders were liking it even less.

The twofold displeasure however didn't show up for a while. Advani even hosted the capital's cartoonists to high tea the evening before he took over as home minister in 1998. To be fair, he had all along been a keen cartoon watcher and appreciated Abu Abraham, his colleague in the Rajya Sabha and a trenchant critic of faith-led politics. Soon, the calendar came to the cartoonist's help. Official attention turned away from adversarial cartooning towards promotional arts, music and euphoric kitsch in keeping with the mood of the new millennium that was approaching.

With the advent of the 21st Century the country caught up with some of the best global practices of the 20th. One such in pedagogy was the tried and tested use of archival cartoons as curricular material, as a trigger for debate in the class room. A selection of published cartoons from newspaper archives was included in 2012 in the NCERT (National Council of Educational Research and Training) Political Science text book for class 11. Students were beginning to enjoy these and it was too good to last. One Shankar cartoon of 1949 on the proceedings of the Constituent Assembly was seen by MPs as offensive to Dr Ambedkar. The parliament was in session and all parties condemned the long dead master cartoonist and asked for the removal of the cartoon from the text book. The matter could have ended there.

Cartoons Poison the Young

The Union HRD Minister Kapil Sibal asked for a thorough relook at every rerun cartoon and promised the House that all 'inappropriate material' would be removed. One such quickly seized upon by members from Tamil Nadu was Laxman's cartoon on the anti-Hindi public stir of the 1960s. It was instantly judged as anti-Tamil. None told the House that the same Laxman had drawn a stronger cartoon against the imposition of Hindi on non-Hindi speaking regions, which was the very provocation for the public agitation. The cartoon's context which was precisely what the class 11 students were supposed to research, analyze and debate was factored out by the MPs who chose to see every cartoon as a piece of timeless art that must satisfy prevailing norms of political correctness. Little did they realize that if the same norm is applied to cinema, the film archives would have to be emptied.

This kind of arbitrary blackout hardly mattered to students, whose parents were rich enough to buy them

Internet-enabled mobile phones. Proscribe anything and trust the kids to search vehemently for it. And as is wont on the web, they will find more than what they are looking for. The students who were actually deprived were those in the backward regions with low connectivity and access. In an attempt to stop divisive cartoons of caste and language bias, MPs ended up deepening one more divide that mattered to learners—the digital divide. Two MPs refused to join the chorus—Sharifuddin Shariq of National Conference, member from Baramullah and the senior BJP leader Jaswant Singh.[7]

Unlike our parliamentarians who condemned cartoons outright without a second thought, a cartoon scholar and cartoonist, Unnamati Syama Sundar addressed the issue mindfully. The result was a thorough study on the caste bias in cartoons published as a book, *No Laughing Matter, Ambedkar Cartoons 1932 – 1956*. Sundar analysed 111 news cartoons where Dr Ambedkar figured and found clear caste bias in the verbal comment as well as the visual depiction of this stalwart of modern India. It is an incisive unsparing indictment of the cartooning tribe. Interestingly, one cartoon that doesn't get blamed is Laxman's—a reaction to the Electoral Bill that Law Minister Ambedkar piloted to ban government contractors from contesting elections. The author calls the cartoon 'a pretty accurate depiction'.[8]

What is it that insulates Laxman? Could it be that there is an inherent urbanity about his work? Where does that come from? Or is it simply because he doesn't stylize too much? You'd hardly find humans being transformed into animal forms or mustachioed men recast as buxom women in Laxman's cartoons. Such devices are stock in trade for cartoonists but run the risk of laying bare deep-rooted prejudices or causing unintended offence. A simpler factor that helped could be his workplace, Mumbai. The host city set Laxman apart from his peers, most of them in the thick of Delhi politics driven by the hinterland's caste baggage. Not that our West Coast is exactly the left coast or Mumbai casteless. But if you wish to, you can manage to live in this city without caste. The Common Man has.

CITY IN SINGLE COLUMN

Having driven Laxman to Mumbai, Delhi didn't switch off. *The Times of India* had an edition in the capital and the cartoonist was there on the front page. He appeared more regularly in print than most Delhi counterparts, including Shankar, who had become a weekly presence since independence. Amidst the national power shift, the capital's star cartoonist had tried to launch a daily paper but had to settle for a cartoon weekly. *Shankar's Weekly,* however, was quick to pick up a high institutional readership across the subcontinent.

The weekly seldom had occasion to feature Laxman. When the country's best-read satire magazine folded up in 1975, the farewell souvenir had just one odd cartoon by its most loved cartoonist.[1] By then Laxman had reached saturation exposure elsewhere. New readers came whenever *The Times of India* opened new editions. Where the flagship didn't reach,

The Illustrated Weekly of India filled in. This big-paged periodical processed and displayed art work on quality paper, unlike *Shankar's Weekly*, elegantly laid out but printed on brittle newsprint. Laxman illustrated stories, including those by his brother R.K. Narayan, caricatured celebrities and cartooned on themes that went beyond everyday politics.

Black Ambassador

The epicentre of the cartoonist's fame was Mumbai. The city became integral to Laxman in a manner few cities have been to a cartoonist. The West Coast port town gave him work, attention and early stardom. Trend tracking Bollywood was quick to turn to the rising star. Guru Dutt commissioned Laxman to draw the cartoons for his 1955 film *Mr & Mrs '55*. Dutt played the protagonist, a struggling cartoonist.

A large concentrated urban readership seemed to have taken to Laxman instantly. In cartooning, often overlapping generations of practitioners create a tide that lifts many boats. Here we see a considerable cartoon loyalty emerge around a single newcomer. That too in a city whose primary concern is commerce, which then and now makes less news than politics.

Mumbai was however professional enough to see cartooning as a regular career, not as a mission or hobby. Laxman saw the point and set out to be a regular office goer like his typical reader. In many respects readers saw the cartoonist as one of them, rather than a wisecracking know-all with higher access or authority. The only luxury Laxman allowed himself was exemption from rail commute. He drove to work and back in a black Ambassador car. Over the decades he owned model after upgraded model of the same brand, always black. Once when Hindustan Motors, the car company, had only a white one in stock, the story goes that it met the loyal customer's order by repainting it black.

Every once in a while the black car would take Laxman and wife Kamala to evening parties with social contacts from multiple vocations. Here was a facial, gestural pool the cartoonist could dip into whenever he had to cast characters outside the pale of power politics. When State Bank of India commissioned him to do its annual calendars he had his banker models ready. To do a hospital scene, he had a range of doctor types to choose from. There were professorial ones who absentmindedly strayed into his *Science Today* cartoons. His lawyers, businessmen, hoteliers, whiz kids, culture vultures and the sundry professionals that make up metropolitan life could well have been culled out of these long evenings.

Soon a shadow was cast over these happy gatherings by a thin stern man. Morarji Desai became the Chief Minister of erstwhile Bombay and decided to uplift the city morally. He banned all things that corrupted minds, from alcohol to crossword puzzles. Laxman hit back with a stiff caricature and stuck to it for life. Even when the long-time Congressman's fortunes changed dramatically enough to usher him in as the country's first non-Congress PM, Laxman kept the mould unchanged—gaunt, disapproving, non-smiling killjoy. Such a merciless character freeze is unusual in his work. His Nehru, Indira, Rajiv, Kamaraj, Karunanidhi and Jayalalitha have all changed over the years. The only other character he cast in iron was the one he created, the Common Man who was anything but a party pooper or killjoy. From the occasional onlooker in the display cartoon, the character graduated to the pocket cartoon as protagonist. This gentle being became the very bond between his creator and the city.

Everyman for Every City

The Common Man could be more accurately called the City Man, though his wardrobe lagged. After early attempts at dressing to please the colonial eye—suited, booted and capped—he settled down to the familiar form in dhoti and checked coat. It reminds one of the sartorial transformation of Gandhiji from barrister to Bapu. Laxman's Common Man stopped short of baring his chest.

Standing out in the anachronistic dress code, Laxman's character is very much part of the metropolis. Even when you sight him in a drought-hit village, he is clearly on a visit accompanying some official or minister. His natural habitat seems to be the characteristically crowded urban Indian space. A compulsive doodler, Laxman could easily do a crowd scene, which he did without creating clutter. This is precisely how Mumbai functions. Hordes of people are moving around all the time; everybody is in a hurry and knows the other is in no less. In the milling crowd in Churchgate or the Crawford Market none bumps into you as in a Delhi bus or a Kolkata tram. Private space is possible. Nothing exemplified it more than the single column rectangle that greeted you on your Mumbai mornings.

'You Said It' seemed to reflect the city. At least this was the constant feeling it created in the readers. They would swear by the day's cartoon and tell you they had been in that very lampooned situation the other day. And long-time loyalists would testify that the daily pocket is the best visual chronicle of the city. Take a closer look and it is then that you realize that the cartoonist was a master illusionist. To begin with he never drew Mumbai into the cartoon. No identifiable part of the city was sketched. You won't see Church Gate, Gateway of India or Chowpatty in the pocket cartoon's backdrop. If this master at travel sketches didn't create a sense of place in the day's cartoon, it can only be because he chose not to. He knew how Mumbai powered his art and his readership. He knew no less that both had to eventually outgrow the city. Brother R.K. Narayan had shown the value of a lifelike literary locale that isn't geographically limited, Malgudi. 'You Said it' was Laxman's own 'Mega Malgudi', a vast Mumbai-like metropolis, not quite Mumbai.

As *The Times of India* started new editions, the new readers in Pune or Ahmedabad found nothing specific in the cartoon's space to suggest a city other than their own. This non-committal visualisation cut across as the paper went to Kolkata, Bangalore and Chennai, helped in no small measure by the cartoonist's reputation that travelled ahead of the editions. Ultimately, every city that housed a new edition saw the pocket cartoon as its own reflection and greeted the Common Man as the guy next door. Laxman had virtually created a national urban comic prototype. Both the character as well as the setting, equally evasive on specifics had much that was portable. Laxman could derive a common minimum subset out of the famously maximum city he worked in.

Far from reductionist, the subset itself was open and welcoming, which is how India saw Mumbai. It was the dream city for migrants from all over. People stream in looking for a living and the big life. Over the decades this sprawling, towering, bustling metropolis resisted being the proverbial crucible that melts all; Indians from every part of the country live here. In effect Laxman got read by a national readership, a lot more representative than in any other city, including Delhi. His newspaper expanded to new regions and by the early 21st century had an all-India footprint. Did the marketing guys compare notes with the cartoonist? Unlikely, because he was a formidable presence in the office. But right through, the cartoonist's vision remained in singular sync with the business plan of the publisher. Perhaps even a bit ahead of the curve.

The Silent Man Fluent in English

By the turn of the 20th Century, Laxman was speaking to a morning crowd that couldn't have got bigger for an Indian cartoonist. Like the other big brand of Mumbai, Lata Mangeshkar, over half a century, the tone never wavered, the pitch was steady and there wasn't an off-key note. In fact, not even a shrill note. More than screaming news breaks, broad news trends were essayed. Politics appeared obliquely. The comment was softly packaged into an abundant visual. Detailing cushioned the barb. The punch was on occasion pulled but the plot was never lost. This fine tuning was done and delivered day after day.

This pocket cartoon was indeed a grand oddity in terms of both language as well as location. Quietly ignoring Gandhi's vision that India lives in its villages, Laxman went and located it farthest from the village, in a big city getting unsteadily bigger. It is doubtful if there is any pocket cartoonist in the history of the art who had to address so mixed a readership, in such numbers, in a link language that was neither his nor theirs—English. A creative contemporary of his, Satyajit Ray, chose to chronicle India mostly through his first language, Bengali. Laxman didn't know much of Marathi or Hindi, the two major languages of his host city. He was most comfortable in Tamil, Kannada and, of course, English.

Like most white collar expats he worked in the English language in an Indian setting, a predicament the cartoon mirrored. 'You said it' sought to generate situational humour which meant the setting looked straight out of life and the soundtrack matched. The visual was like a grab from CCTV footage. There was an unfinished feel to it that made it look more live than schematic. There was nothing sleek or stagey about it. It took much draftsmanship to pull it off across the two-inch tile in print. None in the frame was posing for the cartoonist or the reader. Often you had to look hard to find the protagonist, the familiar bewildered figure, lurking in the background. There are occasions when the visual plot plays out in the background, dwarfed by a clumsy banister or a cluttered table top in the foreground.

The language had to go with the casual air. More than written text, the caption sounded like spoken language. Laxman hardly ever wrote a memorable gag, never a catchy one liner, unlike some of his peers. Sample these stand-alone gags. Abu Abraham: 'Ideologically, what are you – RIGHT, LEFT or Youth?'[2] O.V. Vijayan: 'Lessons of history, General. MILITARY takeovers don't last – only POLICE takeovers do.'[3] Laxman's captions instead look casual and rambling. When asked why he couldn't write shorter captions, his reply was, 'That's the way Indians speak'. Whoever spoke in the cartoon gave you the impression of thinking first in the mother tongue and then delivering it in English. That was how free India's first generation migrants learned their working language. Laxman tropicalised the pocket cartoon.

The single column pocket cartoon, a French favourite, was brought to England by Osbert Lancaster and then on to India, not by Laxman, by Samuel. Delhi-based T. Samuel in 1953 introduced 'This is Delhi', arguably the country's first pocket cartoon in *TheTimes of India*. It was such a big hit that across the new border of the partitioned subcontinent, it was pirated in Pakistani newspapers as 'This is Lahore'. Samuel's everyman was Babuji, a clerk in our early self-government, after whom the feature was eventually renamed. Beyond Babuji, his wife Bibiji and the daily bicycling commute between home and work, Samuel had little to add. He was constrained by a hierarchical and access-controlled Delhi, where an office clerk had limited mobility. Laxman's Common Man with an undefined job role was a far more portable character in a functionally fluid Mumbai. You could follow him into a wider world.

CAPITAL BEFRIENDS, UNFRIENDS

Cartoonist O.V. Vijayan called it the sharpness of the expat. What made the cartoonist detached and intense at once, he thought, came thanks to migration and what it brought—displacement and longing for the lost home. He should know. He was a migrant himself and so were most of his peers in Delhi. Mumbai was a bigger destination for the nation's job seekers and it had Laxman.

Our early cartoonists loved to draw the train. Their best annual economic statement was on the railway budget, more than the bigger union budget. It was their ritual thanksgiving to the iron horse that brought them to the big city. The city and the cartoon have a shared history. The comic drawing has long been the bridge between the first generation migrant and the host city's newspapers.

Cartoon historian Judith O'Sullivan explains how this happened at the turn of the 19th century in the emerging American cities.[1] 'The Sunday Funnies,' as the early American comic strips were called, became a huge hit with the migrant workers. They were picking up English. In their journey from semi-literacy to a working knowledge of the host language, what endeared them most was the clumsy English spoken by comic characters in the cartoon strip. Below the blissfully informal and minimally grammar-bound speech balloons, these characters engaged in exaggerated gestures that completed the communication.

For the first generation immigrants to America's big cities, Sullivan says, comics were entertainment and education. Learning happened with no intimidation. The speech balloons were handwritten to begin with and seemed fallible enough to comfort the learner. They looked chattier than the rest of the paper that was mechanically typeset.

At the close of the 19th century there were phases when comics single-handedly drove newspaper circulations in the US. Legendary press barons, Randolph Hearst and Joseph Pulitzer waged market wars over the first comic strip, The Yellow Kid. Over the years, the readership grew, comics grew and the American city grew into a great production centre and marketplace for comics. The relatively young nation that laid claims to a legacy no more hallowed than Christopher Columbus circa the 1490s, had no qualms about accepting this low art as a major art.

In India it is Laxman and his Mumbai that came closest to this bond between the cartoon and the metropolis. Mumbai welcomed every kind of business, including the entertainment industry. It is home to Bollywood and knows how to make stars out of its entertainers. It valued its satirist no less and the satirist on his part was no less entertaining. The front page newspaper cartoon grew on Mumbai like a leisure page comic.

The Surrogate Comic Strip

'You said it' is a panel cartoon that works like a surrogate comic strip. If you ask a cartoon historian what makes a comic strip a success, the one word answer would be, 'character'. Striking characters, who—over the years—do nothing out of character. This is applicable to Laxman's pocket. To find a protagonist wasn't easy when he started out. Comic art was already familiar to Indian readers. Clones of the *London Punch* magazine had had a good run in several pockets in northern and western India. Lucknow had the *Awadh Punch*, an Urdu satirical weekly from 1877 to 1936 and closer to Laxman's terrain in Bombay Presidency, *Parsee Punch*, a weekly comic in English and Gujarati, was in circulation from 1854 till the 1930s.[2]

Laxman's readers must have already known how cartoons speak—through recurring characters. The usual suspects in the comics cast must have all been tried out—impish child, grown up bungler, adventure freaks, super strongmen, mythological characters and sundry ghosts. Every stereotype must have had its run. To find a new comic figure of appeal for the metropolis' biggest English paper was truly a task.

Laxman says the man found him. It is a story he likes to retell. In his early cartooning days it was customary to have a crowd of onlookers watch the political action unfold in the foreground. The background cast was to represent the divergent India and was quite a nuisance to ink in under a killing deadline. Laxman let the crowd melt away and it did, leaving behind this man in dhoti and coat. This is like the proverbial sculptor chipping away all but the residual figure from a piece of rock.

By the time he emerged, however, the Common Man was already a bit of a relic in a city on the move. Here is where Laxman didn't make the kind of anxious mistake a lesser cartoonist would have. He had the confidence of the long-distance runner. He did not update the man's look or feel. The Common Man stayed on in the dated checked coat. On the rare day he played truant, the absence in the vintage wear was doubly noticed and there was a clamour by readers to bring him back. Amidst the everyday flux, Mumbaikars were in no mood to give up this one sign of ritual permanence that went with their morning coffee.

Like the protagonist, the setting underwent little updation. Laxman has been criticized for his stock visualization of outdoors like city streets and the countryside, as well as the interiors of offices, science labs, hospitals, schools and colleges, all of which are stuck in 1970s or thereabouts. If he didn't indulge the emerging progeny of his own settled readership, it is because of a certain faith in his time-tested art practice. He knew that retro is no less an appealing fashion mode. Asked why his common man hasn't changed in all these years, he shot back, 'Change? Does the colour of the sky ever change?'[3]

Like the sky, the character's basic task was to be there. Always. He appeared without fail, did little to advance the central plot in the drawing and stayed silent all but once. In a 1954 sequential cartoon, when harangued on a visit abroad over India's claims on Kashmir and Goa, he reminds the host about the west's hegemony over Kenya, Malaya and Cyprus.[4] After this singular outburst, the man lapsed back to a lifetime of silence. The Common Man's wife is more forthcoming and does speak out quite emphatically. It would seem that when the cartoonist wants a forthright comment to be made he brings her in. The standard fare however, is a lot quieter—situational irony, with much left unsaid.

Laxman created reader loyalties unparalleled in India and comparable only to the best of American comics, each of which stood out. Charles Schulz's 'Peanuts' has a flavour and humour all its own, quite apart from 'The Wizard of Id' or 'Calvin & Hobbes'. Much like Western Classical music, where the soprano and alto stick to their ranges, Laxman functioned within a practiced and perfected emotional bandwidth. Through days of big bad indifferent news breaks the cartoon never showed anger or despair. It didn't provoke you into fighting authority, but told you to always distrust it.

This mild-mannered cartooning glory was eventually noticed in Delhi. When the going was good the capital rewarded the cartoonist amply. Padma Shri, Padma Bhushan and Padma Vibhushan—every state honour came to him barring the highest, the Bharat Ratna. Historian Ramachandra Guha tweeted in 2015 that more than many contemporaries, Laxman deserves the top civilian honour. When times got tough, the state turned hostile—for what it perceived as good reasons.

How Silence was Censored

The Laxman cartoon grew on the aspiring professional classes as part of urban living. When the cartoon itself, as we saw, got portable enough to work in any city, then the voice of dissent could spread. This could be tapped by an imaginative opposition or could hurt on its own. Delhi at its insecure worst woke up to this danger. When Indira Gandhi declared an internal emergency in June 1975 and censorship of the press was introduced, the cartoon from Mumbai got special attention.

The Censor could handle the evidently oppositional cartoonists of Delhi, even okay the odd one to generate a feeling of overall fairness. How else could one justify the clearance given to Abu Abraham's famous cartoon of the country's President Fakhruddin Ali Ahmed signing away ordinances from a bathtub? *The Indian Express* was allowed to print it in December 1975, a mere six months after the new restrictions came into force.

The irony was that a milder Laxman was a bigger problem for the censor than a politically explicit Abu Abraham, whose drawing was minimal and the caption said it all. The Abu cartoon left you in no doubt over who was being targeted over what. Laxman instead was oblique and ironical. To begin with there were too many elements in the picture; there was no knowing whether some subtle message was hidden between lines. And the protagonist wouldn't utter a word. How do you interrogate a silent man? The censor took the easy way out and stopped even an innocuous cartoon that had a lady wearing high heels. Was that an allusion to PM Indira Gandhi? You could never tell with Laxman. Officials are mortally scared of the unknown. They found the easy way out by axing cartoon after cartoon.

As if this wasn't enough, Laxman was summoned by the then Information & Broadcasting Minister V.C. Shukla and threatened. The cartoonist was told that he was no exception. His celebrity status would not deter the government from sending him to jail. What went unsaid was the truth of the matter. More than the cartoon's content, what scared Delhi was its impact. The Emergency regime knew that the Laxman-signed cartoon was the kind that could sway Mumbai and similar urban spaces. Indira Gandhi could manage rural votes, or so she thought. What seemed critical in those 19 months of state excesses was middle-class acceptance. Laxman's rectangle was a vital urban interface. The censor's task was to sanitize the cartoon space till it raised no laugh. Every peal of laughter was at the state's expense.

Laxman knew there was little he could do to remain on the right side of the censor. The more innocuous the cartoon looked, the more suspicious Mr Shukla became. The cartoonist went on a vacation to Mauritius from which he hoped not to return in a hurry. But sooner than he and the nation thought, elections were announced and the voters threw out Indira Gandhi and her muscular ministers. Laxman did a couple of unusually gleeful cartoons that betrayed long suppressed anger. One showed the Common Man literally delivering the punch and knocking down India's Grand Old Party. Another had Indira and her gang, complete with son Sanjay Gandhi in a pram, moving into impending exile across the Yamuna river, where Muslims were herded at the height of Emergency.

While the Emergency exposed the fragility of the mild-mannered cartoon, it acknowledged cartooning as a potential urban threat. In those non-Internet days, the location and the physical reach of the publication mattered. Not that the regime was much more tolerant outside the Laxman turf. Right in the national capital well before the Emergency, Rajinder Puri faced no less than prime ministerial disapproval. Veteran journalist Kuldip Nayar states this in his autobiography. He was Delhi editor of *The Statesman*, which featured the edit cartoons of Puri. He got a call from J.R.D. Tata, the chairman of the Statesman Trust over a message from the PMO complaining about the vicious cartoons in the paper. Nayar asks, 'What do we do?' JRD says, 'Nothing. Just ask Puri to be a little less vicious.' The matter went no further than that because the people involved were all products of the much-maligned Nehruvian era, which stopped short of killing the mocking bird.

Unlike Nehru, a self-proclaimed cartoon lover, his daughter seems to have had mixed feelings about the art. A couple of weeks before her father's birthday, Indira Gandhi would sneak into the *Shankar's Weekly* office on Bahadur Shah Zafar Marg and spend a couple of hours picking originals to be framed and gifted. Cartoons made a great birthday gift to the democratic dad. No more. Though neither party would have meant it, Delhi had a patronage regime within which the Nehru-Shankar compact worked. The benevolent ruler could pat the dissident on the back. Perhaps it was a good enough beginning. Democracy, like development, was supposed to trickle down gradually in good time.

Post-Nehru, nothing much trickled down. The Laxman cartoon instead drove a trickling up process. Disrespect for authority was seething up and could spread horizontally. There was an inherent danger to this process, over which the top guys were not in control. With rising urbanization and better communication technology, a residual resistance to authority could emerge and politicians were smart enough to sense this. V.C. Shukla could therefore be seen as a farsighted visionary or an alarmist who overreacted. Either way he was close to truth on the power of this visual satire.

The capital's, and indeed the country's, honeymoon with the cartoon was well and truly over with Jawaharlal Nehru. Among Nehru's successors the best you can say is that some have been less hostile to the practice than others. Not one Indian leader has shown the imagination to realize the true adversarial potential of the cartoon art and appreciate it as a demonstration of a robust democracy. The country's cartoonists have somehow managed to keep the show going through thick and thin, a traumatic censorship (1975–77) and sundry brushes with authority.

Delhi is still a major node but no longer the dominant cartooning place. Thanks to the Internet, the locational advantages are diminishing. A young practitioner like Satish Acharya works out of his hometown Kundapur in Karnataka and feels no loss of relevance. On the flip side, the state can any day cut off the lifeline of the smart cartoonist, as it often enough does with the Internet in Kashmir. One can't predict what the future holds for the Indian cartoon but not very long ago it had a fine hour. On 6 December 1992, the Babri Masjid was demolished and for a whole year through 1993 practitioners from across the country worked like a big vibrant editorial mind. Cartoons in English publications and the language press spoke up for Constitutional values day after day, without any evident orchestration. It seemed they were comparing notes telepathically. One big surprise of the year was a Laxman cartoon that shared the same punch line with Rajinder Puri. One can't find two more dissimilar cartoonists from two farther universes but both asked in one voice: Why isn't the politician building the nation, instead of making and unmaking mosques and temples?

CARTOONS AGE DANGEROUSLY

Star cartoonists have a great run in their newspapers till they call it a day. Then it is curtains for a lifetime's work. More so in India where cartoons are published, read, liked, disliked, loved, talked about, un-archived, banished from text books and hardly recalled.

Laxman seems to defy the last predicament. When he cartooned, his reader bonding was singular. He started the single column pocket cartoon 'You said it' four years into his career in *The Times of India* and for the next 64 years it was the certainty on the front page. When he was out of action with a stroke in 2003, the paper ran a pick of cartoons from his archives. Readers found nothing out of place. The front page bond stayed. Cartoons seemed current. It was when the cartoonist resumed work that readers found something amiss. The drawing had taken a hit.

Is Public Memory all that Short?

Now, years after his death in 2015, Laxman's work pops up every once in a while in the social media, gets quickly shared and widely liked. It engages as though it has just rolled out of the rotary press as his cartoons were in the prime days of the printed paper. The decades-old cartoon leaps across and connects to readers, outstripping the day's crop from the current practitioners. That it does so in the new web space is a bigger surprise.

The web is throwing up more than one surprise. For a country like India with no cartoon archives, it is turning out to be the next best thing. Whichever cartoons are uploaded, for whatever reason, with whatever tag, add up to something like an archive, however disorganized. Again, thanks to Google, public memory is no longer that short. Reader attention extends beyond the here and now, though no user will strain too hard to look back. Netizens look for ready connects. Here is where the cartoon, by its very nature a simple link, comes in. And who can simplify more than Laxman?

The newspaper cartoon is no more than the art of the moment. It is not meant to have a shelf life but on the web we find Laxman getting an afterlife. Reruns aren't however, unusual in the world of cartoons but are normally reserved for the classic evergreens that comment on big historic events. You can't read up on the Second World War without at some point coming across the David Low cartoon of Hitler and Stalin rationalizing the joint unholy capture of Poland. Titled 'Rendezvous', this drawing is recalled as a constant reminder of essential state terror and is a half-page spread on the inside back cover of Alan Bullock's classic study of the two leaders, *Hitler and Stalin: Parallel Lives*.[1]

Closer home, Shankar showed Gandhi on the eve of the subcontinent's partition trying hard to stop the India train on rails that diverge to Hindustan and Pakistan. The younger Rajinder Puri bid a touching farewell to the country's first PM with the obit cartoon titled 'Void'—Nehru's familiar facial outline whited out of a grid of innumerable grieving Indian faces. Abu Abraham summed up a subsequent turn of events, Indira Gandhi's Emergency, as an iconic bathtub from where the Republic's President signed away arbitrary orders that bypassed parliament.

From Laxman's considerable repertoire, you can easily pick similar momentous editorial cartoons marking memorable historic occasions. A frequently rerun one has a ministerial figure stepping out of the screening of *Gandhi*, Richard Attenborough's 1982 biopic. 'Apparently,' he says in awe, 'it is a real life story.' More than such big ticket cartoons, however it is Laxman's bread and butter cartoon that reappears on the web. The ones that articulate everyday governance issues like corruption, sloth, unmet electoral promises or endless administrative delays. These are from 'You said it', his daily pocket series, which features no recognizable public figure, only the fictitious Common Man as protagonist.

In cartooning history, comic characters outlive the creator. But it is a bit unusual for a news-driven one to stay on. The Common Man replayed makes a very different impact from the current crop of cartoons. The reader stops at the vintage cartoon to think a while longer and asks why things are bad even after all these years. The authorities are not merely bungling, they seem committed to bungling. Is there a hardened habitual resistance to governance? In an increasingly urbanizing India, the premium is on improvement. There is a sense of hurry and pointed impatience over sloth and inertia. Laxman readers are migrants, many of whom from the under-reported and arguably forgiving Indian villages. They pour into cities and quickly acquire a certain edginess. The country's first city-aligned cartoonist, himself a migrant, shared this irritability with his largely migrant readership.

This very connect could ironically put off today's city dweller. Young India is gathering pace and wouldn't stay loyal to old brands. Laxman himself isn't one that is getting younger. A trendy reader quarrels most with the immediate past. It is the distant past that holds nostalgic charm. Then how come netizens rave about the yesteryears' cartoon? They can't be taken in by the vintage, which isn't much in the first place nor the alleged wisdom that comes with age. In any case profundity is the last thing you expect from the morning cartoon. Cartoons work precisely because they are not heavy and homiletic.

All the same, Laxman is recalled with evident admiration. Fans post his work on social media as 'evergreen' and 'prophetic'. The cartoonist is invariably commended for his uncanny prediction. Laxman in his days made no such claims and had no such intention. He was as content as any other in the business to get the day's work out of the way and go home. He found cartooning an anxious task rather than a moment of epiphany. He sat biting his nails behind a good working desk on which rested no crystal ball.

But then how does the cartoon tick after decades? Each one seems to have a story to tell with subplots in it that no political analyst or investment banker quite foresaw. Let us pick a few at random and rewind.

It's Only the Salary, Sir

Like his peers, Laxman has cartooned enough on corruption to fill a couple of shows. There is one with the minister, eyes shut, extending his hand under the table. This would seem to be the involuntary ministerial gesture when he sights any visitor carrying cash. This time it is only the attendant walking in with a wad of currency notes and he assures the boss, 'It is only the salary, Sir'. The all too familiar English idiom 'under the table' can't be visualized more literally. The stretched palm works with the surety of a well-worn cliché.

Laxman stuck to tell-tale clichés on an issue like corruption. He chose to be direct. It was not as though he had no option to visualize bribe-giving in any other manner. Indian politicians and bureaucrats constantly improve this common practice. Every time the law is half-heartedly hardened, inventive loopholes ensue. There is more improvisation happening here than in our arts and music. A milestone was reached when a bribe giver appeared in 1992 who brazenly owned up to the act and dragged the country's PM in for good measure.

Harshad Mehta, a stock broker, who shook the Bombay stock market, was charged on 72 criminal counts and apprehended. To secure his release, apparently a crore of rupees was carried to the PMO in a suitcase. The claim was made at a press conference in Delhi, where Mehta's men actually lofted the bag before the TV cameras. Cartoonists were quick to seize the metaphoric godsend. The suitcase was all over as synonym of sleaze. Not just cartoons, movies and TV serials recast the accessory as a ready symbol of political deal making.

Laxman showed no more than a passing interest in the prop. He went back to his old way of portraying bribes non-euphemistically. He stuck to the depiction of wads of currency strewn on the floor, spilling out of desk drawers or bundled into cloth bags. Images as old as Thomas Nast's, which require no contextualizing. The 19th century American veteran drew New York mayor 'Boss' Tweed, as a human body with a bundle of dollar notes for a head. The one-word caption summed up the assault: 'Brains'.[2] Laxman stopped short of personifying sleaze like this. He had other ways of rubbing it in. He would bring in the office sweeper looking on at the heaps of cash and valuables, dug out and scattered all over the ministerial chamber, in disdain, showing no inclination to touch what isn't his. He is the guy who votes out scamsters. Perhaps not at every poll but often enough.

Laid to Rest in the Preamble

Here comes another cartoon which should have been shelved for good. A leader, in ministerial regalia, tells visiting pressman, 'Of course, socialism is applicable to us also. But we promised it to the people and we must give it to them first!' This one refers to an idea whose time many thought was over; it shouldn't have made sense to readers today. Socialism became the flavour of 1970s India, when the fledgling PM Indira Gandhi, challenged by party stalwarts, hit back from an assertive left-of-centre stance. Till then socialism was a promise on poll manifestoes or a slogan on placards. When the young PM went on to abolish annual state grants to the erstwhile princely states and nationalized 14 big private banks, the S-word began to bite. Soon the dust settled and the magic word got written into the preamble of the country's Constitution where it was left to rest in peace.

Those were heady socialist days internationally but the concept worked overseas exactly as Laxman envisaged. Our biggest global ally was the Soviet Union, whose rulers ran their socialist republic from ritzy quarters. By the early 1990s, the socialist superpower collapsed and soon in Delhi, PM Narasimha Rao and Finance Minister Dr Manmohan Singh between them freed up the economy from state control but did nothing to edit out the redundant term from the preamble. Our right, left, left-turned-centrist and centrist-turned-right parties continue to harbour socialism like a phantom pain. With the 2008 collapse of global markets, we saw the ultimate irony of investment bankers poring over Karl Marx primers. The egalitarian concept was back in business only in the realm of ideas but not in the lifestyle of India's ruling classes. In the post-pandemic world, economies are likely to look for welfarist thrusts. It is too early to write off socialism and the cartoon that came with it.

The Phone Could get you Into Trouble

A Laxman favourite is the phone that seldom works. There is an early one which shows the good old land phone confined to a small table-top coffin. The idea, as the Common Man's wife tells him, is to treat the dear departed with dignity. The dead home phone isn't abandoned but is waiting for a decent burial. Back then in the 1960s, you cursed your erratic phone but were hopeful that this was among the problems the IIT kids would come in and solve. Telecom technology did advance rapidly and sure enough we got electronic telephone exchanges, long-distance call booths and sleek, cordless and now the cellular accessory.

Indians took to the cell phone as avidly as they took to the polling booth. Soon there were too many phones chasing too little bandwidth. Connectivity weakened so much so that during an election campaign, the union telecom minister was described by his political rival as 'Call Drop Minister' to resounding applause from the audience. Here too the essential problem remained of catching up with growing demand. The old cartoon stayed good. You still hoped bigger resources and higher tech would solve the problem once and for all. And the authorities would be only too keen to speed up matters because it would make them popular. In any case, how long can you fiddle around with a simple phone?

But before you knew it, the phone reappeared in an altogether new avatar—as an instrument of protest. By late 2010 through 2011, the Middle East saw waves of protest which went on to be hailed as the Arab Spring, organized and sustained for weeks through telephonic text messages. By the time the embarrassed authorities woke up and jammed the phones, regimes changed in Tunisia, Egypt and Libya. The story gets closer home, where communication blockade has become a common practice. Despite the prime ministerial endorsement of a digital makeover, local authorities restrict connectivity whenever they sight trouble. The phone user today is as handicapped as the original subscriber of the phone in the coffin. If anything, you are worse off, if you are one of the million students who access their virtual classroom through an Internet-enabled phone.

Here is a case of a straight take on a utility service staying afloat, finding new realms of relevance. The once innocuous cartoon that was originally a mere comment on the laxity of the phone department goes on to address bigger and bigger issues and finally becomes a searing comment on the big state itself. If the cartoon is rerun in sensitive zones like Srinagar today, the cartoonist could be posthumously hauled up for sedition. Laxman cartoons aren't prophetic; they seem to have the uncanny knack to fit into new unforeseen contexts of increasing misgovernance. These cartoons are not evergreen; that would be unnatural. They age, sometimes dangerously.

AFTER A SHORT CENTURY, THE LONG WAIT

Whenever he sat back to reminisce, Laxman saw his life as a journey—a long journey from early childhood in Mysore, of doodling for as long as he can remember. Coincidentally, the cartoon historian Prof. Colin Seymour-Ure (1938–2017) sees the whole business of cartooning in terms of travel and migration.[1] He explains how some of the finest 20th-century cartoonists left homes and converged in London. How the cartoon image itself travels across cultures to make sense in ways seldom linear.

There are multiple parallel journeys that sustained the political cartoon in the last century. Cartoons also travel through time to produce outcomes different from the original intent. We saw how a vintage Laxman cartoon on the dead telephone finds new provocative potential in today's India. Like the best of the lot who practised the art, Laxman's has been quite a journey and it seems far from over.

However, it was not as though this cartoonist was cheered all along the way. One time he was peer reviewed, it was with reservation. As part of a cover story in *The Illustrated Weekly of India*, where he was interviewed at length by Editor Pritish Nandy, his peers were drawn out on his work. The harshest comments came from the youngest, Ravi Shankar. Ravi didn't think of the senior as a political cartoonist at all. The others had more nuanced misgivings on his editorial cartoons. But all accepted his pre-eminence as the country's best ever pocket cartoonist.[2]

Subsequently, there was a harsher outburst against his work. In 2014, at a Delhi session on cartooning in the Indian Language Festival, doubts were raised over the relevance of his cartoons. What was voiced was not the inevitable fading out of the perishable cartoon but a radical shift in public taste. Not that everyone went along with the eclipse of the cartoonist but the idea of a new cartoon reader was sensational. Unlike his peers who spoke for themselves, here was an appraisal on behalf of an anonymous new kid on the block, who was sizing up the cartoon differently.

The case was that Laxman no longer appealed to the emerging Indian reader, who would only settle for pure acid on the political goings-on and not just feeble comments on civic matters. The veteran was boxed into the municipal space and dubbed the pothole cartoonist. The hard-hitting political cartooning was hailed as the way to go and all else was dismissed as weak, outdated, irrelevant illustration. The picture presented was that of a rising young angry Indian reader replacing the stoic sceptical one, who used the day's cartoon as the proverbial safety valve. The new livid readership, it was averred, wants gladiatorial blood spilling satire and nothing less.

Had such a singular readership emerged, it should have been all over the Internet. Despite the rising viewership of web content, there is no evidence of a hardened cartoon web viewer. Today's cartoonists, on their part, haven't picked up the prophesied adrenaline in the air and got particularly ballistic either. Sure enough the Indian cartoon has changed but in ways far more inclusive. There is undoubtedly a marked change in the look and feel of the cartoon, thanks to the use of graphic software, which goes well with the web space. What isn't noticed equally well is the fact that the old hand-done cartoon blends with this space just as well.

Archival styles shine on the screen and on occasion outshine the new. The minimal artwork of Abu Abraham or the rhythmic brush strokes of Laxman throw up the black against the backlit white screen of your laptop or mobile. The picture looks better than anything the best of newsprint ever printed. And for the pocket cartoonist, the net is nirvana. You are free from the vagaries of print, paper and ink. Also, there is the extra option here to click up and enlarge the single column drawing. The web version is an enhanced experience of cartoons old and new. The point is that the hi-tech platform doesn't privilege the new over the old.

Also, in terms of content the current practitioners are as varied a lot as the Laxman, Abu, Puri generation. The generational shift has not been anything half as dramatic as in Britain, from where we got this art. Our cartooning hasn't sprouted a new visceral stream like Steve Bells, Ralph Steadman and Mike Rawson, who far outpaced their World War vintage predecessors—David Low, Sidney Strube and Vicky. We editorialise a lot less aggressively. In any case there is no sign of a dominant single strain that departs radically from the Laxman mode. This is the space into which the vintage cartoon returns without a fuss. A space far less turbulent than Laxman detractors envisaged.

The new readers don't all seem to be bursting in anger. They seem mostly cool and open to a variety of comic content. For the first time in India, news properties are getting a readership that is not just news-savvy but comics-savvy. It is an increasingly comics-friendly readership that is looking at the day's news cartoon. Earlier generations also read comics but they saw the printed cartoon with another eye, as part of the more respectable editorial domain. Being inherently subversive and subaltern, the cartoon has always defied such venerable zones.

This happened in Laxman's lifetime itself. Not far from Laxman's office, S.K. Bobby Kooka, the Commercial Director of Air India, conceived a comic character, the Maharajah, to represent the airline. Umesh Rao of J Walter Thompson sketched the figure. From publicity hoardings and fliers, the extra-courteous lapsed royal amused the onlooker just by being what he was, often slipping in a catchy remark on public affairs. Air Deccan, a new no-frills airline that came up after aviation was opened up for private players in India, thought why reinvent the wheel and reached across to Laxman and got the Common Man himself as mascot. Laxman was also commissioned by Asian Paints to develop a cartoonish mascot 'Gattu', the black and white boy figure with a broad grin who sold colourful paint. Another venture, again outside the news space, that does no less to enhance the country's comics literacy is the Amul topical series of ads whose boy and girl comic pair routinely allude to current affairs. The cartoon keeps crossing borders even in India, where its scope outside journalism has hardly been explored.

Comics-savvy Cartoon Reader

Within the newspaper itself, the comics–cartoon distinction was formally busted by US editors who moved Garry Trudeau's *Doonesbury* from the comics page to the editorial page. While it started off as a Yale University campus strip, this comic went on to be the first comic strip to win a Pulitzer for editorial cartooning. Since then, graphic reporting by the likes of Joe Sacco has further expanded the presence of the cartoon in the news space. The 2018 Pulitzer Prize for editorial cartooning went to an emotionally powerful series, told in graphic narrative form, that chronicled the daily struggles of a real-life family of refugees and its fear of deportation'.[3]

The conventional domain of news cartooning is expanding to storytelling in our times but the idea was piloted way back in Laxman's youth. Surprisingly, one of the early assignments that Laxman got on arrival in Bombay was from *Blitz* to do a narrative comic. It was to create a set of sequential cartoons to retell a crime story—a sensational murder that shook the city. Two convicts jumped jail, stole guns from the arms depot and drove down the Kalbadevi road, shooting at anyone in sight. They were caught and hanged eventually. The editorial brief was to serially narrate the incident. The graphic story was published, but there is no trace of a copy. When it is found, it would be a collector's item that should tell us a few things about the early ways of Mumbai's metropolitan police.[4]

Laxman's narrative urge played out eventually in the novels and short stories he wrote, *Hotel Riviera, The Messenger* and *The Distorted Mirror*. Many of our cartoonists are accomplished writers of fiction. Laxman, O.V. Vijayan and, among the younger lot, Manjula Padmanabhan and Ravi Shankar. It is a mystery why they kept their writing and drawing separate and did not mash them into graphic novels and stories. Meanwhile, readers on their part have taken to the cartoonish long form. For the first time in India an integrated comic art reading is emerging and it has a place for many kinds of the cartoon art, notably Laxman's. Readers surely have individual likes and dislikes but no collective bias against any one kind of cartooning.

If you have grown up with Archies through Abu Abraham to Art Spiegelman, you have a good chance of growing out of hierarchical, compartmentalized perception. You don't bother whether the cartoon is art or entertainment, high art or low art or whether it deals with the pot hole or the black hole. Young minds seem freer and readier to analyse and accept than judge and reject. And more and more of them know English. India could well be the world's largest English reading country. Much of the global comic art is in English and is on the Internet. If amidst this plenty, readers take to Laxman a good 10 years after his death, it indicates something like a persistence of taste. A stern strain to build up when it isn't exactly the best of times for cartooning. Bad days are not due to any dip in cartooning talent but because of 'The Animals Who Govern Us'.

The Animals Who Govern Us

No offence meant. The title refers to a book of caricatures that hit the stands in 1985 and was widely noticed. Sketched in colour using pencil and brush, three French cartoonists Jean Mulatier, Patrice Ricord and Jean-Claude Morchoisne caricatured prominent world leaders including Margaret Thatcher, Ronald Reagan and Fidel Castro as derivatives of birds or animals.[5] The practice isn't unknown to cartoonists. Laxman on his part has acknowledged the spillover of the human form into not just flora and fauna but beyond. 'An active imagination, fuelled by a keen sense of absurdity, could even see the human resemblance to inanimate objects such as old buildings, the shape of bottles in a drugstore, or to certain models of automobiles.'[6] As a self-confessed practitioner of controlled distortion, he made only a limited foray in this direction. His French counterparts however, went the whole hog to pull the animal out of the political animal.

Not every victim was amused. The Soviet leader Leonid Brezhnev (1906–1982) on a visit to West Germany, took offence to his portrayal as an Ukranian bear in *Stern* magazine. Whether the German leadership was as embarrassed as Chamberlain was over Low's cartoons of Hitler and did something about the star guest's caricature is not known. The visiting veteran was too seasoned to expect the Western press to behave as the docile one back home but he seemed a bit too sure of the global might of his state. His confidence was misplaced.

By 1990 the Soviet Union collapsed and the Berlin wall came down. The two momentous events should have made the world a freer place. Far from it. When freedom comes or goes, the cartoonist is the first to know. Right in the US where the press is protected by the First Amendment, for multiple reasons this is the time edit cartoonists began losing jobs by the dozen. 'Editorial cartooning in the '90s, the Clinton era, has been special so far in that nothing special has emerged,' wrote the Pulitzer Prize-winning American editorial cartoonist Dough Marlette (1949–2007). 'As in negative political ads, a certain venality has crept into cartooning, and a clubfootedness. There's no subtlety, no discrimination, no discernment, no selection of worthy targets. All are treated as if of equal weight and everyone is greeted with a sneer.'[7] Marlette's eminent predecessors, Herblock, Mauldin and Conrad out there and their counterparts here—Laxman, Kutty, Abu Abraham, O.V. VIjayan and Rajinder Puri—were past their prime by then.

Broadly speaking, good times seem to have come to an end for political cartooning. An era ended with what historian Eric Hobsbawm called the short century and it seems to be true of cartooning as well. The 20th century, said Prof Hobsbawm, began late in 1914 with the advent of the First World War and closed early with the Soviet collapse in 1990. This seems to be the era that saw the rise and fall of the cartoon as well. The Shankar, Laxman generation lived through the best of these times. They inherited and nourished the art practice seasoned by David Low and his peers through the World Wars and the Great Depression in between. In both wars, highly human intensive, the one-sided cartoon kept up the morale of the country's soldiers by repeatedly targeting the enemy.

The economic distress that hyphenated the wars resonated with visual satire that naturally sided with the underdog. During the collapse of the New York Stock Exchange in 1929, even as the editors talked up the market, the cartoonist tracked the misery on the ground. Can't tell if it was a well thought-out editorial balancing act but amidst a market that wasn't recovering in a hurry, studies point out that more and more readers came to trust the cartoonist who refused to paint a rosy picture.

The blacks and greys in the cartoon documented those weeks and months more accurately than anything else in the newspapers. The outcome of the war that followed couldn't have been happier for the irreverent art. Had Hitler and Mussolini won, the art practice would have vanished from the planet.

The genre thus came tough and tested to the Indian drawing board and ran for a full short century. In the last few decades the work practice has run into problems here and overseas. There are no signs yet of the global gloom lifting for the cartoon, which ironically seems as creatively upbeat as ever. Going by glimpses on the Internet, there is much comic genius at work the world over, a good part of it on the run from authorities. These censored cartoons sneak into the web, which is beyond borders. A truly comic twist. The cartoonist's underground is up in the clouds. Meanwhile millions of English-knowing Indians are browsing the Internet. Even as they watch old and new cartoons from the world over, they are sure to run into the familiar figure in a checked coat. Only, the good old cartoon suddenly looks more offensive, thanks to a hardening state. The Common Man himself however, is the very picture of poise on a long wait for better days.

ENDNOTES

Mysore: Cow and the Crows

1 R.K. Laxman, *The Tunnel of Time: An Autobiography* (Delhi: Penguin Random House, 1998), p. 62.
2 Judgement of the Honourable High Court of Madras by Justice G.R. Swaminathan, 05 April 2018.
3 *Frontline,* Cover issue on R.K. Narayan, The note by H.Y. Sharada Prasad, 18 October 1996: 27.
4 *Tunnel of Time*, p. 41.
5 *Tunnel of Time*, p. 25.
6 *Tunnel of Time*, p. 30.
7 *Tunnel of Time*, p. 53.
8 Face to Face (FTF) with Karan Thapar, video interview, 07 August 2002.
9 *Tunnel of Time*, p. 73.

To Mumbai via Fleet Street

1 Alaka Shankar, *Shankar* (New Delhi: Children's Book Trust, 1984), p. 29.
2 Prof. Barbara N. Ramusack, *The Indian Princes and Their States* (Cambridge University Press, 2003), p. 223.

Rushing to Delhi

1 Ritu Gairola Khanduri, *Caricaturing Culture in India: Cartoons and History in the Modern World* (New Delhi: Cambridge University Press, 2014), pp. 79–80.
2 Alaka Shankar, *Shankar* (New Delhi: Childrens Book Trust, 1984).
3 T.J.S. George, *Ghoshayathra* (Kottayam: DC Books, 2008).
4 Herbert Block, *Herblock: A Cartoonist's Life* (New York: Macmillan Publishing Company, 1993), p. 33.

Common Man and the Crown

1 Dr Dharmendra Bhandari, *R.K. Laxman, The Uncommon Man, Collection of Works from 1948–2008* (Jaipur: Prakash Bhandari Memorial Trust, 2009), p. 11.
2 *The Tunnel of Time*, p. 148.
3 *The Tunnel of Time*, p. 155–56.
4 *R.K. Laxman; The Uncommon Man,* October 1954, p. 114.
5 *R.K. Laxman, The Uncommon Man,* October 1954, p. 115.
6 *R.K. Laxman, The Uncommon Man,* March 1960, p. 138.
7 *The Indian Express*, 14 May 2012; NDTV 15 May 2012.
8 Unnamati Syama Sundar (edited and selected), *No Laughing Matter: The Ambedkar Cartoons 1932–1956* (New Delhi: Navayana Publishing, 2019) p. 284.

City in Single Column

1 *Shankar's Weekly Souvenir*, Under a Portfolio of 'Pocket' Cartoons, September 1975: 198.
2 Private View of 23-03-1976, *The Indian Express,* reproduced in *The Games of Emergency, A Collection of Cartoons & Articles by Abu Abraham* (New Delhi: Vikas Publishing House, 1977).
3 Sundar Ramanathaiyer and Nancy Hudson-Rodd, *Tragic Idiom: O.V. Vijayan's Cartoons & Notes on India* (Kottayam: DC Books, 2006).

Capital Befriends, Unfriends

1 Judith O'Sullivan, *The Great American Comic Strip: One Hundred Years of Cartoon Art*) Boston: Bulfinch Press, 1990), p. 10.
2 For *The Avadh Punch,* see: Mushirul Hasan, *Wit and Humour in Colonial North India* (New Delhi: Niyogi Books, 2007); for *Parsee Punch* see: Mushirul Hasan, *Wit and Wisdom: Pickings from the Parsee Punch* (New Delhi: Niyogi Books, 2012).
3 Dr Dharmendra Bhandari, *R.K. Laxman, The Uncommon Man, Collection of Works from 1948–2008* (Jaipur: Prakash Bhandari Memorial Trust, 2009), p.10.

4 *R.K. Laxman, The Uncommon Man,* p.114.

Cartoons Age Dangerously

1 Alan Bullock, *Hitler and Stalin: Parallel Lives* (London: Fontana Press, 1991), the top cartoon on the inside-back cover.

2 Illustration number 39; The'Brains', which achieved the Tammany victory at the Rochester Democratic Convention. See: John Chalmers Vinson, *Thomas Nast: Political Cartoonist* (Athens: University of Georgia Press, 2014).

After a Short Century, the Long Wait

1 Colin K. Seymour-Ure, 'Drawn and Quartered. How Wide a World for the Political Cartoon?', Hocken Lecture 1996 (The Hocken Library: Dunedin, New Zealand, 1997).

2 'The Uncommon Man: Profiling the Beautiful World of R.K. Laxman, creator of the Common Man,' *The Illustrated Weekly of India*, 29 January 1989.

3 https://www.pulitzer.org/winners/jake-halpern-freelance-writer-and-michael-sloan-freelance-cartoonist-new-york-times (accessed 01.02.2021).

4 *The Tunnel of Time* (New Delhi: Penguin Books India, 1998).

5 Jean-Claude Morchoisne, Patrice Ricord and Jean Mulatier, *The Animals Who Govern Us* (Farnham, UK: Graphic Grins, 1986).

6 *The Tunnel of Time* (New Delhi: Penguin Books India, 1998), p. 15.

7 Doug Marlette, 'Editorial Cartoonists – An Endangered Species', *Media Studies Journal*, 1998: 124–5.

OTHER CARTOONISTS MENTIONED IN THE BOOK

Abu Abraham (1924–2002) (Signed as Abu) Staff Cartoonist, *Shankar's Weekly,* New Delhi, 1951–53. In London, contributor to *Punch*. Political Cartoonist, the *Observer* (1956–66). Pocket cartoonist, the *Guardian* (1966-69). Back in India, political cartoonist, *The Indian Express* (1969–81). Nominated member of *Rajya Sabha,* the upper house of Indian Parliament, 1972–78.

P.K.S. Kutty (1921–2011) (Signed as Kutty) Staff cartoonist, *National Herald* (1941–42), Lucknow; Madras War Review (1943–45), Chennai; *The Free Press Journal* (1945–46), Mumbai. Various publications from New Delhi including *Shankar's Weekly, Hindustan Standard* (1951–86), Bengali language *Ananda Bazar Patrika* (1975–86), *Hindustan Times* (1961–62), *The Indian Express* (1962–69), Bengali language *AajKaal* (1987–97).

David Low (1891–1963) (Signed as Low) *Canterbury Times* (1910–11) New Zealand; *The Bulletin* (1911–19) Sydney, Australia; *London Star* (1919–27), *Evening Standard*

(1927–1950), *Daily Herald* (1950–53) London; *Manchester Guardian* (1953–63), syndicated in *The Hindu* from 1933–63, Chennai, with a break from 1947–49.

Mario Miranda (1926–2011) (Signed as Mario) With Times of India group since 1953. Contributed caricatures and comic illustrations for *Femina, The Illustrated Weekly of India*, pocket cartoon for *Economic Times*. Travelled extensively to sketch US and Europe, besides many parts of India, Karnataka, Coorg and his native Goa.

Ranga Nath (1924–2002) (Signed as Ranga) Delhi-based freelancer for *Shankar's Weekly*, *The Indian Express*, *The Tribune*, *Motherland*. Spot caricaturist with a world record for autographed caricatures.

Rajinder Puri (1934–2015) (Signed as Puri) Contributor *The Manchester Guardian*, *The Glasgow Herald* (1958–59), London. Staff cartoonist for *Hindustan Times*, New Delhi (1959–67), edited and cartooned for *Stir Weekly* (1972–75), quit cartooning during press censorship under national emergency (1975–77). Freelanced for *The Hindu*, *The Indian Express* and *The Statesman*, (1967–2015).

Pillai Keshav Shankar (1902–1989) (Signed as Shankar) Freelanced for *The Free Press Journal* and *Bombay Chronicle* (1927–32), Mumbai; *Hindustan Times* (1932–46), New Delhi, with a 14-month sabbatical in London (1938–39). Founder Editor *Shankar's Weekly* (1948–75), New Delhi.

Sidney Strube (1891–1956) (Signed as Strube) Chief Political Cartoonist *The Daily Express* (1912–1948). Created a protagonist in the editorial cartoon The Little Man to replace John Bull, the figure who represented imperial Britain. Freelanced for *Sunday Times*, *Time and Tide*, and *The Tatler.*

Thomas Samuel (1925–2012) (Signed as Samuel) Staff cartoonist, *Shankar's Weekly* (1948–52); *Times of India* (1952–55), *The Indian Express* (1957–61). Back to *Times of India* and in Hindi *Navbharat Times* till 1975, New Delhi. Pioneered India's pocket cartoon *This is Delhi* in 1953, later renamed *Babuji.*

O.V. Vijayan (1930–2005) (Signed as OV Vijayan and later as Vijayan) Wrote and drew for *Shankar's Weekly* as staffer and then contributor (1958–1975), New Delhi. Staff Cartoonist, *Patriot* (1963–67). Contributed to several publications, including *The Hindu* till 1975. Quit cartooning during the press censorship that came with the national emergency (1975–77), returned to work for *The Statesman*, New Delhi.

Victor Weisz (1913–1966) (Signed as Vicky) Worked for *12 Uhr Blatt* and other German publications from 1928. Fled Nazi Germany to London in 1935. Contributor *Time and Tide* (1937–43), political cartoonist *News Chronicle* (1941–54), *Daily Mirror* (1954–58) and Chief Political Cartoonist *Evening Standard* (1958–66); regular contributor to *New Statesman.*

ACKNOWLEDGEMENTS

Grateful acknowledgement for supporting research: To Indian Council of Historical Research and the Laurie Baker Centre for Habitat Studies.

Thanks for reads, rereads and editorial guidance:

M.K. Das, author and former Editor (Kerala) *The Indian Express*;

Prof K.P. Kannan, developmental economist and Chairman of Laurie Baker Centre;

Sadanand Menon, writer, speaker and arts editor;

Dr Rizio Yohannan Raj, author, CEO and publisher of *The Marg Publications*;

Dr C.B. Mohandas, professor of English and writer;

Venkitesh Ramakrishnan, Chief of Bureau Delhi and Senior Associate Editor of *Frontline*;

Gokul Gopalakrishnan, cartoonist and cartoon scholar.

R.K. Laxman with Mario Miranda and other delegates at a cartoonists' meet in Hyderabad

R.K. Laxman with E.P. Unny